Hebridean Odyssey

Archie MacDonald, South Uist, 1954.

Hebridean Odyssey

*Songs, Poems, Prose and Pictures
from the Hebrides of Scotland*

Edited by
Marion Sinclair

with
Michael Newton

Polygon
Edinburgh

Editorial arrangement © Marion Sinclair 1996
Pages 171–174 constitute an extension of the copyright
pages

Published by
Polygon
22 George Square
Edinburgh

Typeset in Minion and Meridien by
Palimpsest Book Production Limited, Polmont, Stirlingshire
Printed and bound in Great Britain by
Scotprint, Musselburgh

A CIP record is available for this title

ISBN 0 7486 6196 2

For Iain and Mary Sinclair
and Bridget Galbraith

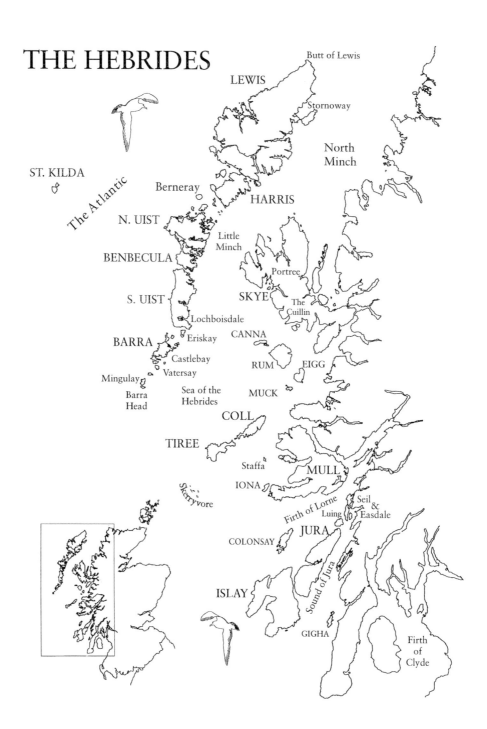

THE HEBRIDES

Butt of Lewis

LEWIS

Stornoway

North
Minch

ST. KILDA

The Atlantic

Berneray

HARRIS

N. UIST

Little
Minch

BENBECULA

Portree

S. UIST

SKYE

The
Cuillin

Lochboisdale

CANNA

BARRA

Eriskay

Castlebay

RUM

EIGG

Mingulay

Vatersay

Barra
Head

Sea of the
Hebrides

MUCK

COLL

TIREE

Staffa

MULL

IONA

Skerryvore

Firth of Lorne

Seil
&
Easdale

Luing

JURA

COLONSAY

Sound of Jura

ISLAY

GIGHA

Firth
of
Clyde

Contents

Contents

*Finlay MacQuien
and Neil Gillies,
St. Kilda.*

Acknowledgements

The editors would like to thank the following for their help and suggestions in putting this volume together: Alison Bowden, Margaret Bennett, Alec Finlay, Ruth Thomas, Ian MacKenzie, Hugh Cheape, Jeanie Scott, Holly Wilson, Neville Moir, The School of Scottish Studies, Edinburgh, and the John Muir Trust.

Foreword

The Hebrides of Scotland have long exerted a hold upon the imagination of travellers. The sense of isolation, the colours, the quality of light, the wildlife, the archaeology, the beaches, the Gaelic language, the traditions and folklore: all are reasons enough to visit and discover this tranquil corner of Scotland. For islanders, the Hebrides are quite simply 'home', a notion which stretches its meaning beyond place of birth and upbringing. This book attempts to explain what that notion means.

Hebridean Odyssey gathers together the elements of a rapidly vanishing culture, using, as far as possible, the words of islanders themselves. The oral tradition of the Gaels has meant that their experiences, opinions and thoughts have not always found their way into print in the past. There is however a wealth of material to choose from and it is hoped that the songs, poems, stories, oral histories and photographs in the book will impart a little of what was and still is special and unique to life in the Hebrides.

Marion Sinclair
Edinburgh, 1996

*Skye Crofters
planting potatoes.*

SKYE CROFTERS PLANTING POTATOES. 5758. G.W.W.

List of plates

Photograph acknowledgements

Photographs on pages 104 and 120 come from the book *Hebridean Images* by Iain MacGowan FRPS and are reproduced courtesy of the photographer. Photographs on pages 9, 10, 20, 28, 48, 76, 84, 88, 109, 112, 128, and 169 are reproduced courtesy of the School of Scottish Studies and Iain Mackenzie. Photographs on pages 4, 64, and 68 are by Gus Wylie and are reproduced courtesy of the photographer. The photograph on page 1 is reproduced courtesy of Comunn Eachdraidh Nis. Photographs on pages 14, 15, 36, and 96 are from the George Washington Wilson Collection, reproduced courtesy of Aberdeen University Library. The photograph on page 132 is by Paul Strand and entitled *Tir A'Mhurain, South Uist, 1954*, Copyright © 1962, Aperture Foundation Inc., Paul Strand Archive; the photograph on page ii is by Paul Strand and is entitled *Archie MacDonald, South Uist, 1954*, copyright as before. The photograph on page 53 is reproduced courtesy of the Scottish Ethnological Archive. Photographs on pages 60 and 72 are from Margaret Bennett's private collection.

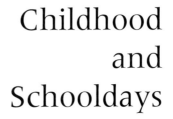

Childhood
and
Schooldays

Johanna MacDonald,
Ness, Lewis.

Angus MacLellan (b. 1869)

South Uist

We mostly lived on potatoes and fish then. We used to have bread and tea in the morning, potatoes and fish for our midday meal, and porridge and milk for supper. There was not much meal coming to Uist then, compared with today. There were few houses without a quern. When meal became scarce with us, we used to harden part of our grain and grind it in the quern. That was the way we lived.

We were beside the sea, and there was no work to be had, and the only way you could get on was to take to the sea itself. I and everyone else in the family went away, and my father and my mother were left alone; when they grew old, I had to come home to be with them. I got on all right after I came home, things were not so hard as they had been at first; we were getting plenty of meal now, plenty of ships were coming to Lochboisdale, but as I first remember, only one ship was coming a week.

The light we used to have was fish livers melted down and burnt in lamps called 'cruisgeins'. There was no paraffin coming to Uist at all, nor word of it. The first paraffin lamp I remember coming here, the smell of it could hardly be endured at all, it was so strong. I think the kind of paraffin there was then was stronger than the paraffin today. There was a man at Peninerine called Ruairi mac Dhòmhnaill Òig, 'Rory son of young Donald', who had got a jar of paraffin. One night he was putting oil in one of the lamps. They weren't very well acquainted with paraffin, and however it caught, the jar went on fire, and Rory began to shout 'My God! Upon my soul! Paraffin! Put it out of the house!' He hardly managed to get the jar out of the house, and nearly set the house on fire before he did! It was a long time before he would allow paraffin there at all, the 'cruisgein' was back again, until the family grew up; when the lads grew up, they made him stop using it. That's the kind of light I remember seeing at first, there was no word of electricity or of Tilly lamps at the time.

from *The Furrow Behind Me: the autobiography of a Hebridean Crofter* (1962)

Finlay J. MacDonald

Harris

Like a lot of people I still have a slight horror of walking into a crowded hall, and, for me, I think it started that moment when my father deserted me inside that schoolroom door. Sixteen pairs of eyes seemed to be tearing me apart as if they were trying to recognize a stranger inside the new Harris Tweed suit which my mother had finished making for me just the night before, and when I attempted to twitch a cheery little smile there was no flicker of recognition from the boisterous boys and girls – some of whom I had been playing with yesterday. When I was beginning to wonder what had transformed them all into a crowd of zombies, I was given my first clue. There was a bellow from behind me, followed quickly by a vicious tug of my left ear and I was spun round to stare into the knees of Miss Dalbeith's hand-knitted stockings. I didn't have time to ponder that I had never seen a strange woman's knees before, or that Miss Dalbeith was ahead of the fashion charts, because a scalping tug of my fore-lock and another stream of English incomprehensibility took my head back and my face up to meet her spectacles. What did dawn on me was that Miss Dalbeith and I were going to have some difficulty understanding each other, because, while I had enough Gaelic to last me for the rest of my life, she didn't have a word of Gaelic in her head.

Schoolroom in Vatersay in the 1970s.

I would willingly have solved the language problem for her by slipping off home – but she was a resourceful woman. She led me by the forelock to the end of a five-seater desk where there was an empty seat beside a girl. She patted the wooden seat first, and then mine. She said 'sit' and pressed me down hard, and so I learnt my first word of English as if I were being groomed for Crufts. From a slot in the front of the desk she extracted a wooden framed slate which she presented to me along with a thin slate pencil and she signalled that I should occupy myself in silence while she proceeded to harangue Primary Five which consisted of one boy called George. I had always envied George his skill in shinning up the telegraph poles which were beginning to sprout in our village. Now I envied him his apparent mastery of the English language.

The schoolroom was square and high and green and yellow. On one wall there was a huge faded parchment map with vast areas of red on it which I learnt in time to be the British Empire. There was a variety of jaded posters, only one of which I remember because of its manifest absurdity. It showed scantily clad, floppily bosomed women up to their knees in water cutting corn, and it didn't take much education to recognize that it was fake. Putting aside the artist's eye for colour completely, I knew that our women would rather die than be seen in that state of *déshabille*, far less cut corn in weather like that. I forget which member of an upper form later informed me loftily that they were Javanese women harvesting rice, but it still seemed to me to be unsound agricultural policy. In one corner of the room there was a round iron object which I jaloused to be a new-fangled stove because of the pipe which led up from it to the ceiling. Beside it was a blackboard on a four-legged easel – at least it had been black once but pale patches were beginning to appear on it like elbows through a jacket, and Miss Dalbeith seemed to spend most of her time scratching words on it for George to repeat over and over again. Her own desk and high chair stood below a window which never closed winter or summer, and on our side of the room there were ten long desks each of them meant for five pupils; but seven of them had been vacant for many years.

There was a great tedium in not knowing English, so I spent some time scratching surrealistic pictures on my slate till the thing was full. I was wondering what to do about it when the girl beside me leant over confidentially and indicated that I should spit on my sleeve and rub. I did, and, lo and behold, the slate was like new. That was the second useful thing I learnt in school that morning, but I was to pay for it a few weeks later when Miss Dalbeith caught me at it and decided to teach me the word 'hygiene' with a cuff on the ear for every time I got it wrong. She was fanatical for hygiene, and in all the time I knew her, I never saw her use a handkerchief. Instead she ripped a piece from an old copy of *The Glasgow Herald* kept specially for that purpose . . . which she trumpeted into and then ceremonially burnt in the round black stove.

from *Crowdie and Cream* (1982)

Catriona MacNeil

Barra

My very earliest recollection of going for a *cèilidh* was with my grandmother. She would take a glowing peat from the fire with a long pair of tongs and, holding it at a safe distance, while I clung to her skirt at her other side, we set forth into the inky darkness. The breeze sent sparks flying from the peat, which to me was most exciting, and I enjoyed the few yards walk to the neighbour's house.

I would be given the treat of a spoonful of sugar in a twist of paper, and I made that last for ages by licking it a few grains at a time. Can I expect any child of today to believe this?

Later we had the more conventional torches and my brother Neil taught me the Morse code so that we could stand at a distance from each other and send messages with the torches. It was great fun. Neil also had a friend in the isle of Vatersay who used to 'talk' to him in the same way. It was a very useful means of communication, especially when bad weather prevented a boat from crossing. Any special items of news were exchanged across the water – a kind of bush telegraph.

from *Only the Sunny Days* (1988)

Peigi Stewart

A 1920s childhood in Skye

When we were little we used to go down to the bottom of the croft and watch my father's boat, sailing out of Uig Bay and going out around the headland. He used to go down, north from here I believe, and sail up the Minch. My mother would never go on the boat, no, oh not while they were fishing. But when they were younger I'm sure she used to go out for a day's trip or day's pleasure. He was at sea quite a lot.

My mother had everything to do because my father went cod-fishing in the springtime from about February, till about April. Well, it was a very busy time on the croft because the cows would be calving and they would have to be fed, kept in and fed and watered – hot drinks made for them, warm drinks anyway, during the day. And my mother used to do all of that on her own, with toddlers around. Well, by that time we would have been at school.

When you went to school, of course, you had no English?

That's right. No, we didn't have any English, but the minute we went to school we were given a book with our ABCs in English and we'd just have to start and learn it all. But in the playground it was Gaelic all the time and English in the classroom.

Interior of Ewen Morrison's house, Lochmaddy, 1938.

Kate Ann MacLellan (b. 1933)

North Uist

I was brought up with my grandmother. She didn't have a croft. It was just a small cottar's house she had. A small thatched house. It had two bedrooms and a kitchen. Outside, we were drawing water from a well. We had no electricity. First of all, we had an oil lamp, then we went on to have a tilley lamp, and eventually, we had a gas light.

The way of crofting is different. When I was growing up, the work was done with horses and ploughs. Now it's all done by tractors. Silage is becoming the thing. In my day it was scything. The men would be out scything and the women were binding after them. They were milking cows in those days, and they were doing butter and cheese, and feeding the calves from buckets.

My grandmother used to go down to the seashore and take a lot of dulses and seaweeds and things home and make different dishes with them. Nobody does that now. She used to take home winkles and cook them and put them into white sauce. Sometimes they were fried with oatmeal. Limpets were cooked and the juice that came off them was strained and put into bottles and used for medicine. And large white shells – I couldn't really tell you the proper names for them – she used to collect those. They were just empty shells which came up into the shingle and she would collect them and boil them and make lime water out of them. That was used for several things including worms in children.

She used to take home dulse, which was very sweet tasting. We'd eat it raw, or she would boil it in milk. And in February and March, there was another kind of weed which you just twirled round your finger to take it off the rock. I just can't remember very well the recipe for that, but I know it was washed several times to remove any sand and put into a three-legged cast iron pot and she kept beating it with a wooden spoon until at last it was in liquid form when it was cooked. And that was drained and bottled and it had a lot of iron in it. So if you were run down or listless, it was used for that.

from *Island Voices* (1992)

Angus Peter Campbell

South Uist

The first image I ever saw was that of a red speckled hen pecking at some wispy straw. It was brought to us courtesy of Cailleach nan Cearcan ('The Poultry Lady') who toured the Western Isles in the late fifties with a slide show aimed at converting the crofters to the wonders of poultry production.

It was, I suppose, an inauspicious introduction to the glittering world of images. My one consolation may be that the red speckled hen and the other forgotten images of that evening of a quarter of a century ago were at least ethnic and authentic.

At about the same time less ethnic but more memorable images arrived in Uist. These were the real 'Pictures' which began to be shown each Saturday night in the church hall at Daliburgh courtesy of the Highlands and Islands Film Guild.

I particularly remember setting off one fading Autumn evening to walk the eight miles to the church hall to watch the latest adventures of Roy Rogers. Half a mile from our home I was given a lift in Domhnall Nellie's car and as we drove along the bumpy road he switched on the car wireless – the first time I'd ever seen or heard such a phenomenon. I remember that Radio Luxembourg was playing, and I became so absorbed by the music emerging from the wavering red dial that I have forgotten the no doubt wonderful Hollywood images of later that evening. That incident serves to remind us that, in the right circumstances, radio can be much more powerful and memorable than film or television.

At school also the memorable images were those associated with that which was strange and distant. We read story books on Friday afternoons and as the schoolmaster dozed and smoked his brier pipe we formed images of places and wonders far removed from Garrynamonie: *Treasure Island, Coral Island, Black Beauty*. All the books told of distant lands and great adventures, and all of them – with the exception of one – were in English.

The exception was *Laithean Geala* by Murchadh MacLeoid. But even that title sounded wonderfully romantic to us – *White Days* – and inside, it told happy tales of sun-soaked days on the shieling in Lewis: secure images which seemed to contrast somewhat sharply with the constant rain and frequent disappointment that seemed to beset us in Uist. This place where boys played in blue rocky pools and lambs gambolled in the white cotton grass became as wonderful to us as *Treasure Island* itself, and because of *Laithean Geala* I had, until my late teens, an image of Lewis as a far-off sun-soaked island where boys and girls and collie dogs played on the shieling all Summer long. The introduction of Comhairle nan Eilean (The Western Isles Council) and one visit to Stornoway soon put paid to all that nonsense.

from *As an Fhearann/From the Land* (1986)

Angus Peter Campbell

Uist 1958

Printed frocks are all I see
and that swift sunshine,
that swift swift sunshine.

Your hair a haystack of curls
in the Garrynamonie morning,
and a green bicycle going softly by.

Shouts, distant calls,
rusty drums and leather balls.

A peewit called,
a school bell, a square bus went by.

A gorgeous print frock by a stone wall.

Uist 1960

Cycling,
you could see them miles away
in the still haze of that Uist day.

Strangers
glittering with silver wheels
and red headbands and green pouches
and a lovely wave as they travelled on.

A soft hiss, a soft hiss,
and the sun caught the spokes as they climbed,
and the hiss, and the hiss, and the hiss,
and the hiss became a distant cow.

Oideachadh Ceart

aonghas macneacail

nuair a bha mi òg,
cha b'eachdraidh ach cuimhne

nuair a thàining am bàillidh, air each
air na mnathan a' tilleadh a-nuas
às na buailtean len eallaichean frainich
's a gheàrr e na ròpan on guailnean
a' sgaoileadh nan eallach gu làr,
a' dìteadh nam mnà, gun tug iad gun chead
an luibhe dhan iarradh e sgrios,
ach gum biodh na mnathan
ga ghearradh 's ga ghiùlan gu dachaigh,
connlach stàile, gu tàmh nam bò
(is gun deachdadh e màl às)

cha b'eachdraidh ach cuimhne
long nan daoine
seòladh a-mach
tro cheathach sgeòil
mu èiginn morair
mu chruaidh-chàs morair
mun cùram dhan tuathan,
mu shaidhbhreas a' feitheamh
ceann thall na slighe,

long nan daoine
seòladh a-mach
sgioba de chnuimheagan acrach
paisgte na clàir,
cha b'eachdraidh ach fathann

A Proper Schooling

aonghas macneacail
Skye

when i was young
it wasn't history but memory

when the factor, on horseback, came
on the women's descent from
the moorland grazings laden with bracken
he cut the ropes from their shoulders
spreading their loads on the ground
alleging they took without permit
a weed he'd eliminate
were it not that women
cut it and carried it home
for bedding to ease their cows' hard rest
(there was rent in these weeds)

it wasn't history but memory
the emigrant ships
sailing out
through a fog of stories
of landlords' anguish
of landlords' distress
their concern for their tenants,
the riches waiting
beyond the voyage,

the emigrant ships
sailing out
a crew of starved maggots
wrapped in their timbers,
it wasn't history but rumour

cha b'eachdraidh ach cuimhne
là na dìle, chaidh loids a' chaiptein
a sguabadh dhan tràigh
nuair a phòs sruthan ra is chonain
gun tochar a ghabhail
ach dàidh an sgalag
a dh'fhan 'dìleas dha mhaighstir'
agus cuirp nan linn às a' chladh

cha b'eachdraidh ach cuimhne
an latha bhaist ciorstaidh am bàillidh
le mun à poit a thug i bhon chùlaist
dhan choinneamh am bràighe nan croit
gun bhraon a dhòrtadh

cha b'eachdraidh ach cuimhne
an latha sheas gaisgich a' bhaile
bruach abhainn a' ghlinne
an aghaidh feachd ghruamach an t-siorraidh
a thàinig air mhàrsail, 's a thill gun òrdag a bhogadh
le sanasan fuadach nan dùirn

cha b'eachdraidh ach gràmar
rob donn
uilleam ros
donnchadh bàn
mac a' mhaighstir

cha b'eachdraidh ach cuimhne
màiri mhòr, màiri mhòr
a dìtidhean ceòlar,
cha b'eachdraidh ach cuimhne
na h-òrain a sheinn i
dha muinntir an cruaidh-chàs
dha muinntir an dùbhlan

it wasn't history but memory
the day of the flood, the captain's lodge
was swept to the shore
when the streams of rha and conon married
taking no dowry
but david the servant
who stayed 'true to his master'
and the corpses of centuries from the cemetery

it wasn't history but memory
the day Kirsty baptised the factor
with piss from a pot she took from the backroom
to the meeting up on the brae of the croft
not spilling a single drop

it wasn't history but memory
the day the township's warriors stood
on the banks of the glen river
confronting the sherriff's surly troops
who marched that far then returned without dipping a toe
clutching their wads of eviction orders

it wasn't history but grammar
rob donn
william ross
duncan ban
alexander macdonald

it wasn't history but memory
great mary macpherson
her melodic indictments,
it wasn't history but memory
the anthems she sang
for her people distressed
for her people defiant

agus, nuair a bha mi òg
ged a bha chuimhne fhathast
fo thughadh snigheach,
bha sglèat nan dearbhadh
fo fhasgadh sglèat
agus a-muigh
bha gaoth a' glaodhaich
eachdraidh nam chuimhne
eachdraidh nam chuimhne

and when i was young,
though memory remained
under a leaking thatch,
the schoolroom slate
had slates for shelter
and outside
a wind was crying
history in my memories
history in my memories

Under the Pier

Ian Stephen
Lewis

It was a green world we went in, under the pier.
Up there above, the dockers caught ropes
and metal boxes that had been tied to lorries
swung over the pier with vegetables and fridges
and wool and chocolate biscuits.

We never walked when we went under but
chased a way down ladders of weedy metal
and then leaped. But no-one ever
fell in, that we remember.

It would have been a disgrace that, if
anyone's slip of a sandshoe had sent them
to splash the greenness into wetness.
We would have been surprised: halted
the game surely and then swapped looks
copied from schoolteachers, ones that said,
'I'm disappointed in you.'

The Land
and the Sea

*Messrs. MacKenzie
approaching Handa, 1935.*

Reminiscences of a Scalpay
Fisherman

Malcolm MacSween, born on 27 July 1881 in Scalpay, Harris, followed his father into fishing at the age of seventeen. After three years at the home fishing he started going to the East Coast for the summers when he was twenty.

How did you get that work? How did you find boats?

Malcolm: People would send word here that they were looking for crews and . . . say I was used to the east coast – if I was well known among them, you know, I might get a letter long before the time came to leave, asking me to go to them. And maybe they needed two more, and could I bring two others with me? And that was how we managed, and other times you'd leave without hearing of anything and as soon as you got there, the people would know when these folk were leaving and they would be looking out for them, and they would speak to them there and take them into boats. No-one would go home without getting a berth at some stage, what with Banff, Portknockie, Findochty and Buckie. And there was nothing going but boats with sails. And what sails! But there was steam on the boats for hauling in the nets, for pulling the rope, and there was steam for hoisting the sail and for raising the mast. Without it nobody could ever have hoisted the sail. Nobody could ever have raised their mast without steam. They were so big and they were so heavy.

Before steam came I suppose the boats were smaller?

Malcolm: Before steam, before steam began there were only small boats, and people managed with their hands. And when fishermen began to make progress, they began to get big boats. And say I built a boat this year and you were going to build a boat next year, I have to build the boat I am going to build bigger than yours, bigger than yours, getting bigger, getting bigger. Finally they got to sixty foot keels and they would be over eighty feet overall. And there was a cabin aft, with bunks, and each man had a bunk to himself, and they were terribly comfortable. And steam took the weight of everything. But people did what they could, if it was only hauling – we used to haul in sixty-five or seventy nets by hand. And if they had herring in them we had to shake that out and clean them.

What did you do then during the winter?

Malcolm: What we did was, we had boats ourselves at home and . . . there was no fishing here in the summer. Then, when the herring started [to come into] the sea-lochs we used to go there with the boats. And, I was on a loch in Skye, at the south end of Skye, called Loch Slapin – a lovely big loch it was too – and there was a big hulk there taking the herring [to cure], and the herring was so plentiful there then and – there were no ring-netters there – and the price we got for a cran was seven shillings. And, we were there for a month, and to tell you the particulars, the day we left home we took a boll of meal, a pound of tea and a stone of sugar, and I was the one – I was young then, and it was my job to cook, make bread and bake it against the stove – big thick oatcakes, an inch thick. That was my job every night. And when we had set the nets we dropped the anchor, and I would bake the oatcakes and everything, and it was herrings and tea and oatcakes, that was our diet. There was no word of cake in those days. And we spent five weeks there from the time we left home until we came home, and I got £24 in money and a barrel of salt herring for myself for the five weeks, and that was quite something in those days . . . £24 then was as good as £80 today. Maybe even better.

Did you go ashore?

Malcolm: We didn't go ashore at all. We would go ashore for anything we ran out of, sugar or tea, but – And we finished a boll [ten stone, approx. 63.5 kg.]

of meal too and we took another two stone on board, and there I had baked a boll of meal plus two stone for them.

How did you bake it?

Malcolm: I had a big tin basin on board and – I could make it today the same way as I made it then. I could make a flour bannock on a table the same as any woman. But it was oatcakes, you wouldn't get to make a bannock there, you didn't have a place to bake a bannock. I just had a toaster made of wire up against the stove. There was a little stove aboard, and I had a toaster like that, made in a shape that would stay up against the stove and bake the oatcake up against that. And, they were good too.

What did you put in it?

Malcolm: Nothing but warm water, a wee drop of warm water in the meal, and no soda or anything went in it but that, but the meal was good then, it was healthier than it is nowadays. And no-one complained of stomach-ache, no-one complained of headaches, no-one complained of anything.

And you lived on oat bread and herring.

Malcolm: Oat bread and herring.

From *Tocher*. Interviewed by Morag MacLeod, School of Scottish Studies.

Jim Crumley

St Kilda

It should begin gently, or at least as gently as St Kilda will permit, for it is an arduous place for muscles and sensibilities, and takes surprising toll of both. If you have time to linger, and if you can resist its forlorn appeal, leave the village alone for a few days, because you cannot begin to understand the St Kildans without first beginning to understand their landscape.

The landscape conditioned everything – the peculiar nature of their own evolution, physically, psychologically, perhaps even spiritually; the way they hunted, the way they built; the nature of the challenge which the rest of us came to find irresistible; even the nature of the weather, for this landscape makes its own.

There are no short miles on St Kilda, and no easy prizes. For all the modest scale of the hills they all begin at sea level and climb either steeply or impossibly. Mostly the hills have no 'other sides', only sea cliffs, so that the view of the hills around Village Bay, for example, is a stupendous sham, a masterly St Kilda deception, a brilliant bluff. Only by crossing north-west into Gleann Mór can you have anything like a hill walk as most people would translate the expression. Otherwise, you climb, not to a hilltop but to a clifftop. To follow the course of fulmar or gannet to the sea from one of these, or to home in on the dwindling wheeling tiers of birds for a thousand feet is to be made head-spinningly and uncompromisingly aware of St Kilda's vertical scale. That is why it should begin gently.

The Gap is a good place to begin. It is not a gap at all, but the head of a corrie with no back to it. The climb from Village Bay is modest by St Kilda's standards, but the essence of St Kilda is immediate, pungent and heady.

You climb amid the simplistically brilliant architecture of the cleits, stone-and-turf storage chambers for seabirds – the St Kildans' daily bread – and other necessities of mid-Atlantic life. They built cleits all over the island, and even on Boreray; some in the most bizarre locations imaginable, some whose locations are as unimaginable as their purpose. Their genius is in a design which sets nature to work, persuades nature to outwit itself, and serve the purpose of man in the process. In that respect, the cleits are a unique achievement, for nature is not easily outwitted on St Kilda.

Four sheep fanks – or cultivation enclosures, possibly both – lie in the lap of the hill, thoughtfully sited, unerringly built with a lack of respect for conventional shapes which accords the stonework an almost pliable air. The St Kildans' skill with stone is evident everywhere, but they built to rude rather than beautiful effect, their dykes rarely straight or circular, as these four fanks testify. One of the four is itself in four sections without a single geometrically identifiable shape among them.

The villagers built with what was to hand, so that you have to look to incomers and late comers and their influences for buildings which do not echo the natives' instinctive sympathy with their land.

There is an ambience around the fanks with at least the illusion of circling hills, the satisfying landscape aesthetic of the single curve of Village Bay and Oiseval, and the hypnotic silhouette of Dùn beyond, all of which seems somehow to have stored best the St Kilda of the St Kildans. It is not something which is easy to explain, and it is not as simple as shuttering the army camp from view, for your mind soon learns to do that as the landscape exerts its own influences. Perhaps it is nothing more than the evidence of the St Kildans' artless art and its unfailing sense of place. Prospects behind and below are so compelling that the Gap, when you reach it, comes not so much as a shock to the system as an unwillingness to believe your eyes. The map warns you that it all exists, the edge-of-the-world cliffs, the seaward miles to Boreray and its stacs, but there seems no good reason to believe it, and certainly no reason at all to believe it could all look like this.

Three things happen at the Gap to dislocate sensibilities. The first is that your hill-girt world which has wrapped the climb in well-rounded heathery securities (dash of merlin, monotone of snipe, underfoot glimmer of orchids) suddenly stops. One stride you are on the last pull up a hillside like any other, the next there is no hill left, and the stride after that would leave you in some turmoil 600 feet above the sea with no land beneath your feet. The Oiseval cliffs loom 300 feet higher to your right, the Conachair cliffs 600 feet higher to your left. Below, there are only infinite depths of birds.

The second happening is that you step into one of St Kilda's bird-climates. Fulmars are all around the village, but not like this. Here they wheel around your head, fly past side-headed, hang on the air in long black-eyed scrutinies a handful of feet away, or shake their wings like a garden sieve just above and behind your head so that you spin in expectation of some fearsome unsuspected force and find only the unblinking black eye, the sleek head, the side-slipping grace of fulmar flight. The fulmars nest here in thousands, swarm on stacs and cliff faces and grass ledges and impossible non-ledges, fill the air from clifftop to wavetop. The sitting birds bicker constantly so that there is a vast fractured sound on the cliffs, but the flying birds are utterly silent so that there is an eerie cordon about you, an unbreachable protective shield fashioned from their long looks and their soundless fearlessness.

This capacity of birds, and particularly seabirds, to so dominate hours and places around St Kilda will be one of the abiding memories. They come at you in tides, or stifle the seaward view with their strength in numbers, and muster the one force which can be equal in its visual power to impress with the landscape and seascape. Almost invariably it gathers aspects of that power from the fact that it is allied to the most powerful of landscape elements for its setting. There are 63,000 breeding pairs of fulmars on St Kilda, widely distributed, but it is at the Gap that they celebrate their finest hour.

The third phenomenon of the Gap is that your seaward gaze is magnetised to the prospect of Boreray and its stoical storm-fending stacs, Stac Lee and Stac an Armin. Boreray surprises with its size, especially its height; the stacs with their abrupt ocean-challenge. All three are chameleons of their own micro-climate, making their own mists which shade and shadow their appearance with a grey pallour, a black menace; or in strong sun and in season Boreray is a vivid emerald green above the cliffs. Stac an Armin is forever gannet-white in every weather, but even that stark shade glistens or dulls as sun and cloud and storm make their plays.

Already you feel on the roof of an incredible world, with further horizons than you have ever know, but you are only halfway up Conachair. It has begun as gently as St Kilda permits.

from *St Kilda* 1988

Finlay McQuien,
outside his home, St. Kilda, 1938.

Gaoth Thig a Canaidh

J. L. Campbell

Ghaoth thig a Canaidh,
   Gum fairich mi blàth i;
'S tòil leam bhith coimhead
   An rathad a thà thu;
'S goirid an ùine

Gu'n till mi g'ad ionnsaigh,
Gun d'fhalbh mo chluas-chiùil,
   Cha n-eil sunnd orm ri ceòl-gàire;
'S acain mo ghaoil dhomh,
   Cha n-ioghnadh mar thà mi,
Cumha na h-ògmhnaoi
   'S bòidhche 'san àite;
Cruth mar an sneachda,
A sùil mar an dearca
'S a gruaidhean air lasadh
   Air dhath mhucag àileag.

Nuair théid mi do 'n leabaidh,
   Cha chadal 's cha tàmh dhomh,
'N amm éirigh 'sa mhaduinn
   Gur h-airtealach thà mi;
Théid mi 'nam dheannaibh
Gu Cnocan a' Bhaile,
Choimhead na mara,
   Fiach am faic mi am bàta.

Gun ghuidh mi Di-Luain
   A' ghaoth tuath mar a b'àill leam
A lionadh a bréid
   Gun éirigh le bàirlinn,
Soirbheas gun diobradh
Gun bhagradh le righneas,
Ach rogha gach side
   Gus an tìm sin am màireach.

Nam faighinn ort naidheachd
   Nach biodh tu 'nad shlàinte,
Gheobhainn na feara
   'S gum faradhainn àm bàta;
An seòladh no 'n iomradh
Cha rachamaid iomrall,
Eadar Rubh' Àird-na-Murchainn
   Gun ruigeamaid Àros;
Nuair théid thu 'nad dheise
   Gur deas am measg chàich thu,
'S math thig an gùn dhut
   As ùire bho'n t-snàthaid;
Caol ann an cumadh,
Am fasan a Lunnainn
Bho d' bhrògan gu d' mhullach
   'S leat urram na h-àilleachd.

Nam faiceadh tu 'n iùbhrach
   Is siùil rithe an àirde,
Sgoltadh nan tonnan,
   'S 'gam pronnadh fo sàil;
Bu chianail an sealladh
Air bhaideala geala,
A h-aghaidh air Canaidh
   Mo Anna 'gam fhàgail . . .

The Wind that Comes from Canna

[1]

The wind that comes from Canna, I feel it warm; I like to be looking in your direction; short is the time until I'll be coming back to you; my ear for music has gone, I have no pleasure in the sound of laughter, I sigh for love, it is no wonder how I am, missing the most beautiful girl in the place. Her form is like the snow, her eye like the berry, and her cheeks are alight with the colour of the wild rose-hip.

[2]

When I go to bed, I cannot rest or sleep; at the time of rising in the morning, I am weary. I go in a hurry to the hillock of the village, to look at the sea, in case I can see the boat. On Monday I prayed for the north wind I wanted, to fill her sails, without raising billows, a mild steady breeze without threatening stiffness, but rather the choicest of weather until this time tomorrow.

[3]

If I were to get news that you were not well, I would get men and load the boat; sailing or rowing we would not go astray, between Ardnamurchan Point, until we reached Aros. When you put on your dress you are pretty amongst all others, well the gown becomes you, newest from the needle, slender in shape, in the fashion from London; from your shoes to your head-tip, you have the honour of beauty.

[4]

If you were to see the ship, with her sails raised aloft, cleaving the waves and pounding them under her keel, the sight of her white topsails would be a sad one, her bow towards Canna, my Anna departing . . .

from *Canna: the Story of a Hebridean Island* by J.L. Campbell (1984)

E. Mairi MacArthur

Columba's Island

At no stage in Iona's history will it have been possible to deny the power and presence of the sea. Today, dominated as we are by overland communications, it is easy to forget that for centuries our west coast was a busy maritime thoroughfare. In Colum Cille's time, and as the reputation of his monastery strengthened over succeeding generations, the sea brought a steady stream of pilgrims seeking teaching, healing or absolution. It brought exiles such as Oswald, a prince of Northumbria who sought refuge among the Scots during a time of turmoil and became a convert. When he later gained his throne in 634 he sought a missionary from the Celtic church and so the great centre at Lindisfarne, under Aidan from Iona, was born.

The waters cast up strays from time to time, for example the shipwrecked Arculf who found himself on Iona for a spell during Adomnán's abbacy. The misfortune that threw together this Gaulish bishop and the scholarly island abbot has left Dark Age historians with a rare bonus, Adomnán's book *The Holy Places*. For Arculf had just travelled through the Holy Land and was able to give his eager listener an eyewitness account of what the countries and cities of the Near East looked like, along with myriad details about their social, political and religious conditions. In a wattle cell amid the Hebrides, the Gael and the Gaul talked of the Sea of Galilee, of crocodiles on the Nile, of an icon of the Virgin Mary in Constantinople.

The ocean brought danger too, however. Before the end of the eighth century the Vikings had swept down the west coast for the first time, plundering and killing. The island monastery was a defenceless target and in 807 Abbot Cellach retreated to Ireland to build a new foundation for his monks at Kells. A small community did hold on in Iona. Indeed, the writing of a ninth century

German abbot, Walafrid Strabo, implies that an Irish monk named Blathmac deliberately sought out the island where 'many a pagan horde of Danes is wont to land' and was slain there in the year 825. 'Thus Blathmac became a martyr for Christ's name' concludes the chronicle, provoking the image of Iona as even then a place where it was not only saintly to live and work but also to die.

The island remained exposed to attack and in 849 the relics of Colum Cille were divided, to be taken to Kells in Ireland and to a church founded by Kenneth mac Alpin, probably at Dunkeld. The wave of raids on Iona came to an end with the slaughter, on Christmas Eve 986, of the Abbot and fifteen monks. By then the early timber monastery had been rebuilt in stone and foundations excavated in 1957 below the present Cathedral cloister garth have been tentatively identified as belonging to this period.

Ian Cowie, a member of the Iona Community, has never forgotten watching the archaeologists at work one summer day at the south-east corner of the cloisters as, out into the twentieth-century light, there emerged a skull. Then came several more plus the entire skeletons of seven or eight men. They had died violently. One had his pinkie clamped between his teeth.

Slightly concerned that the young son by his side might be frightened at such a grisly sight, Ian asked if he was all right. A child's curiosity still had the upper hand, however, as he replied without alarm: 'I suppose that's what you call a skullery!' It is not impossible that the 'skullery' was once the chapel where those monks were at prayer, for the last time, that December night in 986. Their remains were given a respectful reburial in the Cathedral grounds.

The Columban monks changed Iona physically, to a degree. Or at least they accelerated a process previous inhabitants had begun, by clearing oak and ash trees for their timber needs and making inroads into the remaining natural scrub of birch, willow, hazel and rowan. There are virtually no old indigenous trees there today. What their monastery and mission set in motion also changed the island in a less tangible, but equally permanent, way. It became 'The Sacred isle', perceived as such throughout the lands which eventually became Scotland and beyond. It could no longer be just one Hebridean island among many. The prince and priest Colum Cille, and by extension Iona itself, have ever since been bound into the national story.

from *Columba's Island* (1994)

Ben Buxton

Cutting Peat on Mingulay

The land provided peat, which had been used as fuel from prehistoric times in the Hebrides. Mingulay was fortunate in having plenty of peat, and there was no restriction on its use, though there was a north-south division of the island corresponding to the north-south division of the village. The peat on the northern promontory (the Ard) was the best. A track which runs along the steep west side of MacPhee's Hill is believed to have been made to ease access for ponies. The Mingulay peat was also cut by the Berneray crofters, who had none on their own island.

Getting peat was a family activity that went on throughout the summer. Cutting began in May. The peat was cut from vertical sections into brick-shaped pieces. The turf was first cut off with a spade, and the peats may have been cut with a special spade which had a blade at right angles to the main one; this was known as a *treisgeir* in Barra, where it was in common use. The waterlogged peats were laid out on the ground for a few weeks for the water to drain off, then laid upright against each other to continue drying. When hard and dry, they were carried down to the village directly; alternatively, they were built into stacks, possibly on the stone 'platforms' which can be seen dotted about in boggy places. The peats could thus be collected at leisure. Those who had ponies used them to carry the peats down to the village in creels, made from rods of black willow known to the islanders as *caol dubh*; it grew on the shores of Loch Sunart on the mainland, and was collected by the fishermen when fishing there. The rods used for the creels carried by ponies and people were thinner and more pliable than those used for lobster creels. The creels had one flat side for ease of carrying on the back, and were held, when carried by people, with one hand over the shoulder, and the bottoms were flat to ease loading on the ground.

The peats were built into big stacks in the stackyards of the houses, thatched with turf. A family might get through eight or nine stacks during the year, for the domestic fire was always kept burning.

from *Mingulay* (1995)

West Bay, Portree.

WEST BAY, PORTREE. 5757. G.W.W.

Hallaig

Somhairle MacGill-Eain

'Tha tìm, am fiadh, an coille Hallaig'

The bùird is tàirnean air an uinneig
troimh'm faca mi an Aird an Iar
's tha mo ghaol aig Allt Hallaig
'na craoibh bheithe, 's bha i riamh

eadar an t-Inbhir's Poll a' Bhainne,
thall's a bhos mu Bhaile-Chùirn:
tha i 'na beithe, 'na calltuinn,
'na caorunn dhìreach sheang ùir.

Ann an Screapadal mo chinnidh,
far robh Tarmad 's Eachunn Mór,
tha 'n nigheanan 's am mic 'nan coille
ag gabhail suas ri taobh an lóin.

Uaibhreach a nochd na coilich ghiuthais
ag gairm air mullach Cnoc an Rà,
Direach an druim ris a' ghealaich –
chan iadsan coille mo ghràidh.

Fuirichidh mi ris a' bheithe
gus an tig i mach an Càrn,
gus am bi am bearradh uile
o Bheinn na Lice f' a sgàil.

Hallaig

Sorley Maclean
Raasay

'Time, the deer, is in the wood of Hallaig'

The window is nailed and boarded
through which I saw the West
and my love is at the Burn of Hallaig,
a birch tree, and she has always been

between Inver and Milk Hollow,
here and there about Baile-chuirn:
she is a birch, a bazel,
a straight, slender young rowan.

In Screapadal of my people
where Norman and Big Hector were,
their daughters and their sons are a wood
going up beside the stream.

Proud tonight the pine cocks
crowing on the top of Cnoc an Ra,
straight their backs in the moonlight –
they are not the wood I love.

I will wait for the birch wood
until it comes up by the cairn,
until the whole ridge from Beinn na Lice
will be under its shade.

Mura tig 's ann theàrnas mi a Hallaig
a dh' ionnsaigh sàbaid nam marbh,
far a bheil an sluagh a' tathaich,
gach aon ghinealach a dh' fhalbh.

Tha iad fhathast ann a Hallaig,
Clann Ghill-Eain's Clann MhicLeòid,
na bh' ann ri linn Mhic Ghille-Chaluim:
Chunnacas na mairbh beò.

Na fir'nan laighe air an lianaig
aig ceann gach taighe a bh' ann,
na h-igheanan 'nan coille bheithe,
dìreach an druim, crom an ceann.

Eadar an Leac is na Feàrnaibh
tha 'n rathad mór fo chóinnich chiùin,
's na h-igheanan 'nam badan sàmhach
a' dol a Chlachan mar o thùs.

Agus a' tilleadh as a' Chlachan,
á Suidhisnis's á tir nam beò;
a chuile téòg uallach
gun bhristeadh cridhe an sgeòil.

O Allt na Feàrnaibh gus an fhaoilinn
tha soilleir an dìomhaireachd nam beann
chan eil ach coimhthional nan nighean
ag cumail na coiseachd gun cheann.

A' tilleadh a Hallaig anns an fheasgar,
anns a' chamhanaich bhalbh bheò,
a' lìonadh nan leathadan casa,
an gàireachdaich 'nam chluais 'na ceò,

If it does not, I will go down to Hallaig,
to the Sabbath of the dead,
where the people are frequenting,
every single generation gone.

They are still in Hallaig,
MacLeans and MacLeods,
all who were there in the time of Mac Gille Chaluim
the dead have been seen alive.

The men lying on the green
at the end of every house that was,
the girls a wood of birches,
straight their backs, bent their heads.

Between the Leac and Fearns
the road is under mild moss
and the girls in silent bands
go to Clachan as in the beginning,

and return from Clachan
from Suisnish and the land of the living;
each one young and light-stepping,
without the heartbreak of the tale.

From the Burn of Fearns to the raised beach
that is clear in the mystery of the hills,
there is only the congregation of the girls
keeping up the endless walk,

coming back to Hallaig in the evening,
in the dumb living twilight,
filling the steep slopes,
their laughter a mist in my ears,

's am bòidhche 'na sgleò air mo chridhe
mun tig an ciaradh air na caoil,
's nuair theàrnas grian air cùl Dhùn Cana
thig peileir dian á gunna Ghaoil;

's buailear am fiadh a tha 'na thuaineal
a' snòtach nan làraichean feòir;
thig reothadh air a shùil'sa' choille:
chan fhaighear lorg air fhuil ri m' bheò.

and their beauty a film on my heart
before the dimness comes on the kyles,
and when the sun goes down behind Dun Cana
a vehement bullet will come from the gun of Love;

and will strike the deer that goes dizzily,
sniffing at the grass-grown ruined homes;
his eye will freeze in the wood,
his blood will not be traced while I live.

Interior of an Island House, 1888

Mingulay

'An old woman at her time-blackened spinning wheel, sitting on a lump of the naked rock beside the peat fire, which is burning brightly without smoke, in the middle of the clay floor; two children healthy and brown beside her, playing with a kitten; a hen mother and some chickens busy foraging for themselves over the clay floor; a small pig scratching his back under the bench of driftwood supported by turf on which we were sitting. A little table, but no dresser; one small chair, one three-legged pot, and a kettle, not to omit the never-failing friend of every old wife in the kingdom, the brown teapot standing by the fire. What more? A quern or hand-mill on the table, in daily use still in an island where there is no population to support a miller, and where the meal is still prepared by two women grinding it painfully in this primitive way. Three stout kists [wooden chests], the property of the girls of the family who had just returned from the fishing at Peterhead. This is about all. Most of the houses have separate byres, which are cleaned out twice a year, but this dwelling was one in which the cows were tied up along with the family in the same end of the cottage in four stalls between the fire and the door. During our visit the cows were in the fields, but there was plenty of evidence to show where they lodged at night.'

from 'Yachting in the Hebrides' by Mrs Murray (1888)

Francis Thompson

The Gael has always been an outdoor man. 'Home' to him was the great outdoors, and his house was merely a convenient shelter from inclement weather. It was not an object of domestic luxury. Rather, it was a building erected to shut out the storm. In good weather it was normal to live out of doors, for instance during the summer months when the folk of the older Highland townships went off to the hill grazings, to the sheilings, which were something of an extension of the home. James Boswell, Dr Samuel Johnson's companion, describing his visit to Coirechatachan, remarked: '*We had no rooms that we could command, for the good people here had no notion that a man could have any occasion but for a mere sleeping place.*'

The house or dwelling place was, however, a focal point of some social significance, as indicated by the Gaelic expression '*aig an teine*' (at the fire), applied to the main room of the building, and suggesting the value attached to the social graces and aspirations of friendship. When the exiled Highlander speaks of 'home' he rarely means his parents' house; rather he means his native village, and, in the larger context, the immediate area of moors, hills, glens and rivers which made up the place of birth. This attitude meant no disrespect to the dwelling where one's family had been born and brought up. But it was ever the case that it was the natural and physical environment, the wider elements of sky, moorland, hills and the like, which provided the basic identification.

This is something which may well stem from the old times when a clan had its identity tied in closely with a well-defined territory.

In these modern times, when planning consent must be obtained for nearly everything, if a crofter builds a new house, the older house must be pulled down. But before the advent of the planner, when a new house was erected the old place was merely put to new use as a barn or store, and was seldom razed. In some cases the old home was left to the rigours of wind and rain and allowed to fall into a tumble of stones, to become some kind of visual reminder of a former time and style of living. In many places in the crofting areas of the Highlands and Islands one sees the older dwellings, now softened by time and weather, standing beside the new structures: neglected and forlorn – but not forgotten.

from *Crofting Years* (1984)

The Crofter's Garden

Thomas A Clark

A sea of kale,
an allotment of waves,
an acre of islands,
a harvest of graves.

TV show makes German laird of Dun Maraig!

Come on down, Stefan ... You've won tonight's star prize – a Scottish island!

Seriously, folks. A young German bank worker has become the owner of a tiny island off the north-west coast of Skye, courtesy of a television game show.

Twenty-year-old Stefan Schluznus, who lives in Verden near Bremen, wrote to the Isle of Skye and South West Ross Tourist Board asking for more information about the island – Dun Maraig, a few hundred yards off the township of Cuidrach south of Uig. This week the *Free Press* spoke to Stefan to find out exactly how he became a Scottish property-owner.

'Meine Show', apparently, is a TV phone-in show which offers a variety of prizes from more commonplace game show offerings like new cars to the more unusual like a farm in Canada or an island in Scotland. 'The last show was in the summer of this year and I was the last winner,' said a clearly-delighted Stefan.

He had the title to the island locked in a vault, but he recalled that the TV company had bought Dun Maraig from an agent in Hamburg who in turn had bought it from 'a collector'. The collector, Stefan thought, was a Mr F Vladi, with offices in Hamburg as well as in Vancouver and Washington. 'This owner collects many islands but he was not interested in my island so he sold it to an administrator in Hamburg,' he added.

Stefan has never been to Scotland, and so far he has seen only a few pictures of Dun Maraig which is about an acre in size and has a ruined fort on it but apparently little else. However, he hoped to visit the island with his girlfriend in April or May of next year.

He said: 'I think – in my dreams – of building a cottage on the island. What we call in Germany a garden house, of wood only. I think it would be nice to sit in it and look at the Atlantic ocean.'

from *The West Highland Free Press* (1994)

Working
Lives

Thatching at the Johnstone's Eriskay.

The Waulking Described

Mrs Morrison

The Waulking Day may now be called one of the institutions of the past. It belonged to the time when the Highland women manufactured their own clothing, and also that of their households . . . The making of fine material, and the designing of beautiful patterns, and the dyeing of the wool into the different shades, was a delight to the Highland women; and to see their husbands and sons arrayed in becoming garments of their own handiwork gave a dignity to many lives that were otherwise commonplace and uninteresting, and gave rise to a healthy emulation among them as to who should make the finest plaid or the prettiest web . . .

It was a great labour to produce a good web. The wool had to be carefully washed, and then finely teased. Then the carding and the spinning and the dyeing had to be gone through, and when the right number of cuts for the number of yards wanted were wound into balls, the proud and victorious owner of them took them to the weaver to have the pattern set. She never went on that mission empty handed. She always took to the webster a cogful of meal, some butter, a kebbuck of cheese, a braxy ham, or whatever in the way of food happened to be most plentiful at the time. This offering was supposed to make him work cheerfully at his loom, so that he would leave a blessing on the cloth.

Every matron and maiden in the township knew when the web was expected home from the weaver's, and they could be heard humming some of the waulking songs that they would be expected to sing. The day came at last on which they were invited to help . . . and shortly after breakfast they gathered at what might be termed the festive house. A table was covered and sumptuously laid with whisky, divers kinds of bread, butter, cheese, and cold mutton, and any other delicacy at hand. The matrons examined the web, and discussed the colours, the pattern, and the texture, while the maidens carried stoups of water, or pails, from neighbouring houses, of a liquid called by them *màighstir* or *mac a' mhàighstir.**

The web was put into a large tub of water and soap, and well tramped. A strong door was taken off its hinges, and laid on rests, so as to enable them to sit comfortably around it, and the web, saturated with the soapy water, was laid loosely upon it, and forthwith the work began. All seemed full of light-hearted gladness, and of bustle and latent excitement, and as each laid hold of the cloth, with their sleeves tucked up to the shoulders, one could see the amount of force they represented ... These good women, with strong, willing hands, take hold of the web, and the work proceeds, slowly at first, but bye and bye, when the songs commence, the latent excitement bursts into a blaze.

The greater number of these songs are tragic, and, in ballad style, have a story in them equal in interest to any three volume novel ... These Gaelic songs were never sung to a listless, uninterested audience. Every face was beaming with interest in every word of it that expressed feeling or suggested sentiment. One [woman] sings the song, while all take up the chorus, weird and plaintive, and as they toss and tumble the cloth, passing the folds from hand to hand, a stranger, who saw them at the work for the first time, might be pardoned for thinking them mad.

from *Transactions of the Gaelic Society of Inverness* (1887)

* urine

St Kilda waulking Song

I would make the fair cloth for thee,
Thread as the thatch-rope stout.

I would make the feathered buskin for thee,
Thou beloved and importunate of men.

I would give thee the precious anchor,
And the family gear which my grandfather had.

My love is the hunter of the bird,
Who earliest comes over misty sea.

My love the' sailor of the waves,
Great the cheer his brow will show.

from *Carmina Gadelica, Ortha nan Gaidheal* (1900)

Fisher girls from Barra, 1929.

John Grant

Skye

A long time ago, there were men who were called 'The Drovers' . . .

It's certainly true that they used to come here many, many years ago. They were the 'real' drovers, they weren't like the drovers that are around today. They'd come from the mainland, probably up from Fort William, and Stirling, and Falkirk, and they'd buy the calves and any of the cattle that were available for sale. There were probably from a dozen to twenty of them, and they always had dogs, they were sheep dogs. These dogs would move out the cattle and keep the cattle together.

They'd keep to the old roads – there weren't any roads then like there are now – and they'd go through the straths and through the glens, and when they'd come to the ocean, such as at Kyle Reay, they'd swim the cattle across to the other side, until they'd come to Glenelg. That's where their journey would start again. They then kept going on the same path, staying with the high moors where it is easy for the cattle to walk, without being too hard. And, at night or in the afternoon, when they would arrive somewhere, they would stay overnight so that they and their cattle could take a rest, and they'd have some food together.

And there would probably be a wee hotel as they had then on the way. They would take a bit of food with them, when they'd leave. It seems that the food that they preferred to carry with them was oatcakes and cheese and if they didn't have any, they could make some 'fuarag'. But 'fuarag' was commonplace for centuries before that. When they were wearing the shoes, they would put a wee bit of water in the heel of the shoe. Then they'd put some oatmeal in it, and if they had any whisky, they'd put some in it. And that kept them going, it was good food that would keep you going for a day.

But if there was a wee hotel, they'd have some proper food there, until they finally arrived at Falkirk. That's where there was a great livestock market. There wasn't anywhere in the Highlands as large as that at all, there were only small places.

They didn't have the kind of cattle we have today at all, but the old cattle, the old Highland breed. They were tough creatures, and good at travelling. Therefore, if they just took it at an easy pace, they could go a long distance in a few days, but they had to keep the pace nice and easy, or else they'd become weak. And if they got weak, they weren't any use at all. They didn't want to leave any of the animals behind them, and so they had to be pretty sure they they were travelling the right path and at the right speed. But these were old Highland cattle, not the animals around nowadays – they wouldn't be of much use at all, I'd say . . .

Brian Jackman

Sula Sgeir

Sula Sgeir is one of the most inhospitable places on earth. A storm-lashed rock, barely half a mile long and ringed by cliffs 200 feet high, it rises from the North Atlantic some forty miles beyond the Isle of Lewis in the Outer Hebrides. Yet every year the men of Ness make the arduous journey from Lewis to Sula Sgeir to gather the strangest harvest. Here, each summer, they risk their lives to hunt the gugas – fat young gannets which are pickled in salt to be eaten during the winter.

These annual voyages to Sula Sgeir – its Gaelic name means Gannet Rock – were born out of long years of need and privation, when all kinds of seabirds were killed and eaten to enable the islanders to survive the harsh northern winters. In bygone centuries, hunting the guga was a necessity; but today, although the birds are greatly prized as a traditional winter treat on Lewis, the expedition itself has acquired the nature of a pilgrimage. Despite the hazards, it has become a ritual of hardship and endurance, a way in which the men of Ness can keep in touch with their Gaelic roots.

The adult gannet is a magnificent bird. With a six-foot wingspan, it glides effortlessly over the waves, looking for sand-eels which are driven towards the surface by voracious mackerel shoals. When fish are spotted, the gannets catch them by crash-diving from heights of up to 100 feet. Their skulls are strengthened to withstand the impact of hitting the water. Their bodies are protected by elastic air sacs and their eyes are placed so as to give a downward as well as a forward view of their prey.

Wanderers of the wide oceans, gannets winter as far away as the coast of West Africa but return in late March to breed in large offshore colonies in the North Atlantic. Of the twenty-eight European gannetries, thirteen are in the British Isles and eight of these are in Scottish waters.

The islanders of Lewis were not alone in their taste for gannets. Even the people of Edinburgh once feasted on gugas which were taken from the Bass Rock in the Firth of Forth. On St Kilda, too, that spectacular group of islands and stacks lying forty miles west of North Uist, not only gannets but puffins, fulmars, guillemots and gulls were eaten, along with the eggs of razorbills, oyster-catchers and eider ducks.

from *Sula: The Seabird Hunters of Lewis* by John Beatty (1992)

Margaret Fay Shaw

South Uist

There were thirteen houses within the radius of a mile beside the sea loch and all had crofts of about five acres of peaty soil. Yet their potatoes produced an excellent crop, and enough oats were grown to feed their cattle through the winter. Each of the crofts had two cows with followers, and six of the crofts owned a few sheep. They were grazed on the hill which was their common land in the summer months and brought back to the shelter of the croft when the harvest was secure. The cattle were Highland or Highland-Shorthorn cross, which can stand the wet and stormy weather. The sheep were a small type of Black-face that is indigenous to the Hebrides, whose mutton is delicious and whose wool is handspun for blankets and tweed, the women not only knitting the socks and sweaters but heavy underwear for the men.

It was necessary for the men to have other work than crofting. Many were part-time fishermen. Lobster fishing was profitable if the lobsters reached London or Birmingham alive. Herring was precarious but could pay well and salt herring was a mainstay of the diet of the people. Others were deep-sea sailors on cargo or passenger ships sailing from British ports to all parts of the world.

The spring work of the croft began in February, when seaweed, used as fertilizer, was cut with a saw-toothed sickle called a *corran* on the tidal islands of the loch at low water of a spring tide. It was bound together in great bundles called *maoisean* and towed ashore at full tide so high that it could be left on the grass verge. The crofters then carried it in creels on their backs to the field, where it was left in a heap for a fortnight before being spread on the ground.

There it was left until black and dry, the new grass showing above it, when the ground would be ready to turn. The fields were too small to use a horse-drawn plough, so the ground was dug with a spade or a footplough called a *cas-chrom*. This primitive-looking implement, whose name means crooked-foot, is of a type that has been used in various parts of the world since man first tilled the soil. The foot of the *cas-chrom* is made at an angle of 110 degrees to the long handle and the point is tipped with iron, which is pushed into the earth by the pressure of the man's foot on the wooden pin at the bend of the *cas*. It enters the ground at a slant, is tipped back and rolled to the side, where it deposits the clod. Though it does not reach the same depth as a spade, it cuts more evenly and without the back-breaking effort. The clods were then broken up with a heavy wooden rake of five thick teeth called a *ràcan*, and the field was harrowed by hand before the oats were sown.

The crofters planted their potatoes in 'lazy-beds' or *feannagan*. The plot was divided into long rectangles five feet wide and, with a rope as a measure, each rectangle was cut with a spade the length of the plot to the depth of five inches, this cutting along a rope line being known as *susadh*. A strip of seaweed three feet wide was spread down the centre of each bed. The crofter then turned a foot-wide clod or *ploc* to each side of the cut with a spade and laid it on the seaweed so that the strip was covered by a foot of earth on each side, with a gap or *taomadh* of seaweed being left exposed. The two-foot-wide ditch or *claise* between the beds would be as deep as two feet to drain the ground, which was largely peat and often water-logged. The potatoes were then planted with a dibble or *pleadhag*.

Much of the work was done on a communal system: the lamb marking, the sheep clipping, when the men used to shear and the women fold the fleeces, and the dipping to control sheep scab, which was required in Uist by law four times a year. In June the peat was cut. The men would take each house in rotation for the days, usually not more than two, that each required for the year's fuel. Six men were needed to cut the MacRaes' peat, and it was referred to as 'three irons' or *tréisgeirean*, which meant that three men would cut and three men catch and lift the peat to the bank. On these days the women of the crofts would gather at the house of the one whose peat was being cut and help prepare a dinner for the men, of mutton or salt herring and potatoes. They would carry buckets of a drink called *deoch mhineadh*, which is cool, clear water with oatmeal stirred into it, out to the moor to refresh the workers. After the peat was cut it was left lying by the bank for a month, when three peats were stood on end with another on top. Later these were gathered to make small stacks until, at the end of the summer, when dry enough for burning, they were carried home to make the great stack by the house for the year's use. The peat in Glendale was of particularly good quality, being black and hard and burning long and well until reduced to a fine white ash. These peats have different names according to their size and position. The long, flat rectangle as it was cut was called *fàd*, the small broken pieces found at the bottom of the peat bed *caorain dubha*.

In midsummer the hay and oats were cut with a sickle or a two-handled scythe and made into stooks in the field until the time when it was carried home to the shelter of the byre, where it was built into great stacks or *mulain*, the tops thatched with bracken and secured with ropes against the winter gales. The potatoes were dug in October and stored in the byre.

The women worked extremely hard. Though the men would return from the sea in early spring to cut the seaweed and turn the ground, the women carried the creels, helped with much of the planting, harvesting and carrying home the peats. They never complained of the scarcity of many things that the townsfolk are unable to do without. Nor in those black depression years did they ever voice the worry for their menfolk waiting interminably for a ship in a far-away city.

from *Folksongs and Folklore of South Uist* (1977)

Katie Stewart, Glenconan, Skye, 1938.

Johanna MacDonald

Lewis

Can you describe the ordinary working day?

Depended a lot on the season. The cutting of the peat, peat-cutting weather was always lovely. This took place around – this is guess work . . . the potatoes were planted around March, that was got over, I think the next was the peat, that was May. And of course the people foregathered, you had a squad. And you paid back – if somebody came to you, you went to that fellow. There were roughly three or four people to every peat knife. One cut the peats and the others flung them out to dry, and they were left till peat weather, usually the end of May – peat weather, breezy and dry and pleasant. Then when the peat were fairly dry, you put them out into small stacks, like a triangle. After that they were stacked properly into big stacks. Sometimes, they were ferried home at that stage, and a huge peat stack made at home. But more often they were stacked at peat bank and carried in creels.[9]

Who dug?

Didn't matter. First of all, of course, a strong man had to cut the turf off the top of the bank. You know, the heather and the grass. An ordinary spade. Then it was tipped down to the base of the bank, and that gave you a kind of foothole in case the place was boggy. As your cutting began you used the real tool for cutting peat, and one person – the men were the ones who cut, and the women flung. But that wasn't necessarily the order. One cut and one flung . . . the further down you went, the better the quality of the peat, so that the ones at the top were cut in bigger slabs and the further down you went, till you got to the very bottom, it was like coal, very good and very dark. Now sometimes when they were left at the peat bank, stacked in the ordinary peat-stacked way, they were just heaped turfs, until they were ready for creeling home. I often think of these women, their good posture – I took the children home during the war [World War Two] – I had to cut the peat myself, well of course somebody had to help me.

Did you help with peat when you were a child?

Oh, I had to help with the short stacking. Not the carrying, oh no, the women did that, and I often think that's why they had such marvellous posture. When I went home during the war, I had to do the carrying, you couldn't carry a creel without standing properly. The creel sat . . . on your waist. The people were used to it – it was better than going to a ballet school – you couldn't do it properly any other way. They were all such beautiful walkers and I'm quite sure that was the training.

Did the men carry peat?

No – oh, no – don't be silly! The men did the fishing. People used to say those men were lazy! They weren't lazy. The thing was that they were kind of like the camels.

When they were at sea, they were in open sailing boats from Monday to Saturday. And on Saturday, they had to dip their nets in something or other called [cutch] to strengthen them, and put them on railings. So that when they came home they slept until Monday morning. Because they had no sleep, no beds or anything [at sea]. They went away early on Monday morning and they didn't get back until late on Saturday afternoon. On Saturday forenoon was the . . . dipping the nets [she is not sure of term, only knows it in Gaelic] that had to be done, then it was hung on fences to dry. Then the men went home to their homes and practically well . . . ate reasonable meals and slept most of the time till Monday because they had slept very little. During the week there was no way that they could have. The accommodation on the open boats, they were just sailing boats, no cabins. The stories around that the Lewis men were lazy. They were not! Meals were mostly hard biscuits, hard-tack. They lived on that and the fish they caught. The herrings were just chucked into a pan. My uncle said you had no idea how delicious herrings were straight out of the sea into the pan.

When the time came for harvesting, for the crofting spring work, my word, they weren't lazy at that because they hadn't yet gone to sea. You see the herrings came in shoals and went around the coast. It was until May, I think, they had their closed time. They weren't allowed to. Then they did the croft work, as much of it as they could, until they went off to the fishing. And often followed the fishing round the coast. Funnily enough, they never went to Orkney – I wonder why not? They went to Shetland which was much further away [probably following the herring].

The fishing girls – those who gutted the herring – they too went to Shetland. And do you know how? In the fishing boats. Girls too went in the open fishing boats, all the way through the Pentland Firth up to Shetland.

from *Country Bairns: growing up 1900–1930* (1992)

Calum Johnston

Barra
On his mother

S he was a very hard-working woman – never idle at all. At that time . . . well, she worked on the croft, of course . . . milked the cows and attended them in everything, and in the evenings she carded and spun and made cloth. There wasn't an idle moment at all in their lives. They were all the same the women at that time, they were all the same, working all the time. Of course, working – that kind of work – they treated as a recreation. They didn't consider it as

Marion Campbell,
Plocrapool, Harris.

work: it was a pleasure to them. They took a pleasure in their work, especially the work of the cloth – the carding and spinning and all that. They had a pride in it, and they took pleasure in it . . . The greatest pleasure that anybody can get is to see the completion of his work and then when they saw a beautiful piece of cloth or tweed after it had been made, well, that was their reward for the labour they had put into it . . .

All the cloth that the men wore was made by the women – by their wives and their mothers. And even the fishermen . . . they always had to get blue cloth and that blue cloth that was made for the fishermen, it was so thick that they never wore an overcoat with it as no rain would go through it. It was waulked for a whole night. You know when cloth is made it has to be shrunk – what they call waulking. Well, for ordinary blankets and the like of that an hour or so's waulking would be sufficient, but for fishermen's blue cloth it was a whole night. They would start the waulking at perhaps . . . six in the evening and wouldn't be finished until ten at night, with songs going all the time they were shrinking it. And well, when that was shrunk to that extent, nothing would go through it. Oh, yes, they had pride in their work . . . the praise of the neighbours, if it was forthcoming, was payment for all their labours.

from *Tocher, 10*

Francis Thompson

There is a whole world of difference between the picturesque villages of the English countryside and the townships of the Highland scene, which are equally picturesque, but not so photogenic. The English settlements have a long stable history of close communal association, and also a history of regulation imposed by the local feudal manor and its lord. The surrounding countryside is witness to centuries of careful cultivation by the toiling villein and serf, and the total encompassing atmosphere is one of slow-moving, almost Utopian, contentment – or, at least, that is the impression the tourist receives. Many Highland townships, on the other hand, while some are indeed of long standing, have a much shorter history, having been created by displacement of populations in the last one hundred years or so.

Many of the present day crofting townships are products of the crofters' immediate forebears, men and women who often had to make the very soil from an alchemic mixture of seaweed and crushed stones, having been forcibly settled on the most infertile, rocky land possible. The crofting townships also have an atmosphere of perpetual change as dwellings, for instance, are re-vamped from the old style of design to the ultra-modern. There are no particular features in the township which show a development from feudal bond to freehold: no village square, no village pub to act as a neutral area for local discussion, no visible memorials to the war dead and none of the outward trappings which indicate a closely-knit social community. Yet, the crofting township *is* a tight social unit, simply because it is the folk of the township who are the dynamic elements; the physical environment is merely a stage-setting.

from *Crofting Years* (1984)

Pastimes
and
Good Times

Postmaster,
Enaclete, Harris.

Martin Martin

Skye

The diet generally used by the natives consists of fresh food, for they seldom taste any that is salted, except butter. The generality eat but little flesh and only persons of distinction eat it every day and make three meals, for all the rest eat only two, and they eat more boiled than roasted. Their ordinary diet is butter, cheese, milk, potatoes, colworts, brochan, *i.e.*, oatmeal and water boiled. The latter taken with some bread is the constant food of several thousands of both sexes in this and other isles, during the winter and spring; yet they undergo many fatigues both by sea and land, and are very healthful. This verifies what the poet saith, 'Pupulis sat est lymphaque ceresque': Nature is satisfied with bread and water.

There is no place so well stored with such great quantity of good beef and mutton, where so little of both is consumed by eating. They generally use no fine sauces to entice a false appetite, nor brandy or tea for digestion; the purest water serves them in such cases. This, together with their ordinary exercise, and the free air, preserves their bodies and minds in a regular frame, free from the various convulsions that ordinarily attend luxury. There is not one of them too corpulent, nor too meagre.

The men servants have always double the quantity of bread, etc., that is given to women servants, at which the latter are no ways offended, in regard of the many fatigues by sea and land which the former undergo.

Oon, which in English signifies froth, is a dish used by several of the islanders, and some on the opposite mainland, in time of scarcity, when they want bread. It is made in the following manner: A quantity of milk or whey is boiled in a pot, and then it is wrought up to the mouth of the pot with a long stick of wood, having a cross at the lower end. It is turned about like the stick for making chocolate; and being thus made, it is supped with spoons. It is made up five or six times in the same manner, and the last is always reckoned best and the first two or three frothings the worst. The milk or whey that is in the bottom of the pot is reckoned much better in all respects than simple milk. It may be thought that such as feed after this rate are not fit for action of any kind; but I have seen several that lived upon this sort of food, made of whey only, for some months together, and yet they were able to undergo the ordinary fatigue of their employments, whether by sea or land; and I have seen them travel to the tops of high mountains as briskly as any I ever saw.

Some who live plentifully make these dishes above-said of goats' milk, which is said to be nourishing. The milk is thickened, and tastes much better after so much working. Some add a little butter and nutmeg to it. I was treated with this dish in several places; and being asked whether this said dish or chocolate was best, I told them that if we judged by the effects this dish was preferable to chocolate; for such as drink often of the former enjoy a better state of health than those who use the latter.

from *A Description of the Western Islands of Scotland* (c. 1695)

Martin Martin

North Uist

The natives are much addicted to riding, the plainness of the country disposing both men and horses to it. They observe an anniversary cavalcade on Michaelmas Day, and then all ranks of both sexes appear on horseback. The place for this rendezvous is a large piece of firm sandy ground on the sea-shore, and there they have horse-racing for small prizes, for which they contend eagerly. There is an ancient custom, by which it is lawful for any

George Bennett, Glenconan, Skye, 1938.

of the inhabitants to steal his neighbour's horse the night before the race, and ride him all next day, provided he deliver him safe and sound to the owner after the race. The manner of running is by a few young men, who use neither saddles nor bridles, except two small ropes made of bent instead of a bridle, nor any sort of spurs, but their bare heels: and when they begin the race, they throw these ropes on their horses' necks, and drive them on vigorously with a piece of long seaware in each hand instead of a whip; and this is dried in the sun several months before for that purpose. This is a happy opportunity for the vulgar, who have few occasions for meeting, except on Sunday: the men have their sweethearts behind them on horseback, and give and receive mutual presents; the men present the women with knives and purses, the women present the men with a pair of fine garters of divers colours, they give them likewise a quantity of wild carrots.

from *A Description of the Western Islands of Scotland* (c. 1695)

William Matheson
Skye

The Blind Harper has left us a sketch of an evening's entertainment in Dunvegan Castle. There was singing (*ceilearadh beòil*), dancing to music played by a fiddler (*fear-bogha*), and a game played on a board (*clàr*) that involved the throwing of dice – apparently backgammon. He does not say so, but it is probable that, as at Duart, the evening came to an end with the household going to bed and the harper playing soft music to lull his listeners to sleep; just as it was the duty of the piper – and this he does say – to rouse all from their slumbers in the morning.

The reputation of Highland chiefs like Iain Breac for unbounded hospitality found special justification at seasons of festivity, or on other occasions that required to be celebrated with much eating and drinking. At such times poets, bards, musicians and entertainers of various kinds came into their own, and travelled long distances in order to be present. We have a description of what took place from one whose father was brought up not far from Dunvegan Castle during the chiefship of Iain Breac, and it may fittingly find a place here. 'When the Hebridean chiefs and captains', he writes, 'returned home after a successful expedition, they summoned their friends and clients to a grand entertainment. Bards and shennachies flocked in from every quarter; pipers and harpers had an undisputed right to appear on such public occasions. These entertainments were wild and cheerful, nor were they unattended with the pleasures of the sentiments and unrefined taste of the times. The bards sung, and the young women danced. The old warrior related the gallant actions of his youth, and stuck the young men with ambition and fire. The whole tribe filled the Chieftain's hall. The trunks of trees covered with moss were laid in the order of a table from one end of the hall to the other. Whole deer and beeves were roasted and laid before them on rough boards or hurdles of rods wove together. Their pipers played while they sat at table, and silence was observed by all. After the feast was over, they had ludicrous entertainments, of which some are still acted in the Highlands. Then the females retired, and the old and young warriors sat down in order from the Chieftain, according to their proximity in blood to him. The harp was then touched, the song was raised and the *Sliga-Créchin*, or the drinking shell, went round.' Here no doubt is the kind of occasion which the Blind Harper often graced with music and song.

from *The Blind Harper* (1970)

James Boswell

Skye

I was highly pleased to see Dr. Johnson safely arrived at Kingsburgh, and received by the hospitable Mr. Macdonald, who, with a most respectful attention, supported him into the house. Kingsburgh was completely the figure of a gallant Highlander, – exhibiting 'the graceful mien and manly looks,' which our popular Scotch song has justly attributed to that character. He had his Tartan plaid thrown about him, a large blue bonnet with a knot of black ribband like a cockade, a brown short coat of a kind of duffil, a Tartan waistcoat with gold buttons and gold button-holes, a bluish philibeg, and Tartan hose. He had jet black hair tied behind, and was a large stately man, with a steady sensible countenance.

There was a comfortable parlour with a good fire, and a dram went round. By and by supper was served, at which there appeared the lady of the house, the celebrated Miss Flora Macdonald. She is a little woman of a genteel appearance, and uncommonly mild and well-bred. To see Dr. Samuel Johnson, the great champion of the English Tories, salute Miss Flora Macdonald in the isle of Sky, was a striking sight; for though somewhat congenial in their notions, it was very improbable they should meet here.

Miss Flora Macdonald (for so I shall call her) told me, she heared upon the main land, as she was returning home about a fortnight before, that Mr. Boswell was coming to Sky, and one Mr. Johnson, a young English buck, with him. He was highly entertained with this fancy. Giving an account of the afternoon which we passed at *Anoch*, he said, 'I, being a *buck*, had miss in to make tea.' – He was rather quiescent to-night, and went early to bed. I was in a cordial humour, and promoted a cheerful glass. The punch was excellent. Honest Mr.

Mrs. John Gillies Snr., spinning outside No. 11, St. Kilda.

M'Queen observed that I was in high glee, 'my *governour* being gone to bed.' Yet in reality my heart was grieved, when I recollected that Kingsburgh was embarrassed in his affairs, and intended to go to America. However, nothing but what was good was present, and I pleased myself in thinking that so spirited a man would be well every where. I slept in the same room with Dr. Johnson. Each had a neat bed, with Tartan curtains, in an upper chamber.

from *Journal of a Tour to the Hebrides* (1773)

Margaret Fay Shaw

South Uist

Of all the islands I'd visited, there was something about South Uist that just won me; it was like falling in love; it was the island that I wanted to go back to. Of course, I was not looking for *islands*: I was looking for a way to live my life. I went first to Lochboisdale and stayed in a cottage with a Mrs Campbell for two or three months, but there was too much English, and it wasn't exactly what I wanted. Donald Ferguson, who was a cousin of Mrs Campbell's, asked us to Boisdale House for New Year's dinner. So we went around to South Lochboisdale, where we had a lovely dinner, and afterwards Mrs Campbell said, 'What about Peigi and Mairi giving us a song?' They came in from the kitchen, and Mairi sang a song which was absolutely wonderful to me; I'd never heard anything like it, and I said, 'Would you teach me that song?' And she said, 'Yes! If you'll come and see me, I'll teach you that song.' 'Right, I'll come!'

A week later I was able to get a boat over the loch, to the south side where they lived. I walked up to this little thatched house with a blue door and I thought, 'This is where I ought to stay, this is where I want to be, if she'll take me.' So I said to her, 'Could I come here and stay? Would you take me as a boarder?' And she said, 'Yes, if you'll be comfortable here, of course I'll take you.' And that was the beginning. I said, 'Well, I have to go home to my sister's wedding, but I'll be back in about six weeks.' And so I went home to my sister Biddy's wedding, and I came back and moved in with Mairi MacRae, and I lived there for four winters and six summers.

Donald Ferguson had a large farm in South Lochboisdale and his big house also included the shop and post office. The two sisters, Peigi and Mairi, were his cousins, their mothers being sisters. In Boisdale House they were the servants: Mairi the laundry maid and Peigi was both cook and dairymaid and ruled over all. She had a young lass to help her, for the work was never-ending; they were up at five in the morning and never ceased until midnight. The farm-hands were to be fed as well as their other cousin, Angus MacCuish, who was in charge of the shop.

I would come to the kitchen in the late evenings when they would all be having tea and there would always be songs. Peigi and Angus gave me one in praise of Uist with a fine tune and splendid verses:

> O my country, I think of thee, fragrant fresh Uist.
> Land of bent grass, land of barley,
> Land where everything is plentiful,
> Where young men sing songs and drink ale.

Then follows the verse:

> They come to us, deceitful and cunning,
> In order to entice us from our homes;
> They praise Manitoba to us,
> A cold country without coal or peat.
> I need not trouble to tell you it;
> When one arrives there one can see – a short summer, a peaceful
>   autumn
> And long winter of bad weather.

This song reminded me of a woman I met on the roadside who said that since I came from America I might know her son who had gone to Saskatchewan: 'The frost is in their bones and they miss the sea.'

My coming to live with Mairi and her son Donald meant that she no longer needed to work in the laundry. She now had a little money to be independent. It was the same for Peigi when she was old enough to receive the pension and came to live at home with Mairi.

They had both been on the mainland where they learnt English when young. Mairi had been with an elderly spinster near Glasgow who had been kind and patient, teaching her by giving a list of things she must take to the grocer, repeating the names of each item. Peigi had had a much harder time. She was sent as a servant to Donald Ferguson's sisters in Edinburgh. Their house was in a row of tall houses, all with white steps. Peigi knew the way home and which house it was – they were difficult to tell apart for her – because in the window there was a white china swan with a plant in it. The cousins sent her to the Pentland Hills, outside Edinburgh, a long way off, with a bucket; there were sheep on those hills, and they wanted the manure for their garden. So they sent her off, and she got lost. She wandered all over the hills, but she got her bucket of sheep dung and started back. It was by then gloaming, and they pulled the curtains which meant that she couldn't see the swan! She was wandering around the streets and met a policeman who recognised her because he was courting the maid in the next house. So he said, 'Where are you going and what's that you've got in your bucket?' She showed him the sheep dung and said that she'd been out on the hills, and he said, 'This is a very dangerous thing to do at night, to go out in the evening like that!' He began telling her that she should never do such a thing and so on. And she finally said in her broken English, 'I can't find my door!' And so he took her home to the house, and the sisters, who were older than she, thought that this was a big joke – very funny. She was there two or three years before going back to Lochboisdale.

Peigi used to go to what they called the 'gutting', as a member of a crew – five girls who went together to herring stations, ports on the east coast of Scotland. There were huge troughs, where the girls would gut the herring and salt and pack them in barrels. Peigi was a wonderful sailor, never seasick, never afraid of the sea, whereas the 'gutter girls' as we called them, were always terrified of the sea and were violently seasick. She told me about going from Lochboisdale down to Oban on a dreadful day. The girls were very frightened – lying on the deck, practically passing out with sea-sickness, and she was singing! She was a wonderful singer; she never stopped singing on land or sea. She sang all the time, and the fishermen were so delighted with her that they tied her to a chair and tied the chair to the mast so that she could sing all the way to please them. And the girls were shouting and crying and bawling, 'you'll take us right to Hell with your songs! . . . We should be praying God to save us', and so on. This she thought was very funny.

Peigi was a tiny wee thing; I felt just huge beside her – and I'm five feet one. Peigi and Mairi had the greatest wisdom, tolerance, cheer, and courage, and yet had so little. They were glad to have nice things, but they didn't expect them. They had enough food, and they took great pleasure in what they did possess. They had no envy. That was their way of life; they were accustomed to it. And of course it was much better in the years I was there than it had been in years before.

from *From the Alleghenies to the Hebrides* (1993)

Hugh MacKinnon

Shinty in Eigg

HM: Oh, they were playing shinty here, you know, right up to, I suppose . . . I think it was in nineteen twenty-five or six that I saw the last shinty match on the beach.

DAM: And you were playing yourself?

HM: I was down there that day right enough, but not much shinty was played. They laid the camans [shinty-sticks] aside and got out a foot-ball. That was what the young ones wanted.

DAM: Yes, but it was on the beach – at Laig?

HM: Laig beach down yonder, yes. But when I was a boy going to school and we were . . . oh, all the time, and even for two or three years after the first war, there used to be pretty good games of shinty. Everybody in the island used to gather at the beach. And you'd get all of them, perhaps, gathered together getting on for midday, about twelve o'clock.

Then two young lads, perhaps about twenty years old or so, were chosen to pick the sides. And this is how the picking was done: these two lads would stand facing each other and the rest of the players would be round about them, or in a bunch, with these two lads standing facing each other. And one of them would throw his caman to the other and he would catch it about the middle of the shaft, perhaps, and then they would work up [hand over hand] on the shaft of the caman to the top. And whoever had the last hand-hold on it, he was the one who had first pick. And this one, of course, would pick the man he thought was the best player of the lot and that man had to go over and stand beside him. Then the other one would pick the next man. They went on picking the men who they thought were the best players until everyone there was divided, half on one side and half on the other.

And then these two lads who had picked the sides would throw their camans in the air and the camans would land on the beach, as we used to call it in shinty *a' bheulag* (forehand) or *a' chùlag* (backhand). The *beulag* was when you were playing holding the caman with the right hand below and the *cùlag* when you were playing holding the caman with the left hand below. But it was the *beulag* that counted and if your caman fell on the beach with the *beulag* facing north, that would be the direction you would be playing. And if the other fellow's caman fell with the *beulag* facing south, that would be the direction he and his team would be playing in, for it was more or less north and south that the beach ran. (Perhaps it was a little to the north-east or the south-west but it was very little anyway.) But it could sometimes happen that both camans would fall facing the same direction. Then they would have to throw them up again and it could be that they might have to throw them two or three times before the camans could be got pointing in different directions. And then if your caman fell with the *beulag* facing north, you went to the south side. The other lot went to the north side. Then the *coilleagan* were set up: it's the *coilleag* we used to call it. As they say in English, a goal.

The one who got the last hand-hold, he had the first pick and he . . . would say *Buail am port* (?'Strike up the tune'). *Ligidh mi leat* ('I'll allow you'), the other would say. And the one who had the last hand-hold, as I said, he picked the first man . . .

But anyway, the goals were set up, one on the south side and one on the north side, and it would be about twelve feet wide they made them. And they would get bits of stones, those who were on the south side, over at the mouth of Abhainn na Caime and those who were at the north end up here at Ceann Daoibbinn, they would get stones there.

from *Tocher* (interviewed by D.A. MacDonald)

Margaret Fay Shaw

Dancing the Highland dances was one of the joys of life in the Hebrides. In Glendale we danced in the kitchen to the pipes of Angus John or James Campbell, or to Donald MacRae playing the accordion, locally known as the 'box'. For more important parties we used to go to the school-house, where there was room for many to gather and dance the favourite country dances, the Petronella, Quadrille and Eightsome Reel, and to shake the house with the lively Scottische and the old dances native to South Uist. Sometimes it was necessary to walk more than five miles to these dances, and ever-memorable was the boundless energy of Màiri Anndra, who would dance all night and walk the long road home to put on the kettle and begin her daily tasks while her companions lay stretched on their beds too tired to remove their shoes.

from *The Folksongs and Folklore of South Uist* (1977)

Eric Gregeen and Donald W. MacKenzie

Among elements of continuity one must place first the remarkable passion for bardachd which has always been widespread in Highland communities and which manifested itself in almost every aspect of work and social life. Laborious tasks like rowing and cloth-waulking were accompanied by songs. Songs were composed to celebrate birth, marriage, love and death, and to record the incidents of everyday life. And the most characteristic form of recreation was to meet in the 'ceilidh-house' in the evening to pass the time in talk, story-telling and song. So much did song pervade life in the township that it appears to have been as essential as eating and sleeping.

It was not simply a passive enjoyment. The passion for songs was accompanied by an ability to sing and often to compose songs.

from *Tiree Bards and their Bardachd* (1978)

Heatherhouse, Islay.

The Shieling

Alexander Carmichael

Lewis is the only place in Scotland, probably the only place in Britain, where the people still go to the *àirigh* (moorland shieling or mountain pasturage). Throughout Lewis the crofters of the townland go to the shieling on the same date each year, and they return from it on the same date each year. The sheep and cattle know their day as well as do the men and women, and on that day the scene is striking and touching: all the *ni* (flocks) are astir and restless to be off, requiring all the care of the people to restrain them and keep them together and in proper order. Should any event, such as a death and burial, cause the people to postpone the migration, the flocks have to be guarded day and night, or they would be off to their summer pastures by themselves.

Most of the shielings are several miles, some six or eight, some twelve or fourteen miles, from the townland homes. The moorlands are rough and rugged and full of swamps and channels, and the people use much care in guiding the cattle, especially the young ones not yet experienced in travelling. Even these, however, soon learn, being 'gey gleg in the uptak,' very quick of apprehension. It is instructive to see the caution with which the older animals travel over the rough channeled moors, daintily feeling their way when not sure of their ground. When they reach their camping ground the cattle and sheep soon spread themselves over the heather, being tired and hungry. While being milked the cattle eat the fodder which the girls and women have brought in creels.

The shieling time is the most delightful time of the rural year, the time of the healthy heather bed and the healthy outdoor life, of the moorland breeze and the warm sun, of the curds and the cream of the heather milk. The young men come out from the townland in twos and threes and half-dozens to spend the night among the maidens of the shieling; some them play the pipes or some other instrument, and the song and the dance and the merriment begin and are continued all night long under the moon on the green grass before the shieling door. I have heard old men and women waxing eloquent over these lightsome days and nights of their youth and again sobbing and sighing over awakened memories too tender for words.

from *Carmina Gadelica, Ortha nan Gaidheal* (1900)

Francis Thompson

In older times, the *ceilidh* was more than just a gathering of neighbours to talk over local problems and discuss the import of whatever national news might have filtered through to the township via an itinerant packman or tinker. It was also the occasion when memories were revived, when the lineage of the folk of the township was re-stated, when the bards and singers were given the chance to freshen up old songs and poetry with yet another airing, and when the young were gradually made aware of their responsibilities to their families and to the community at large; and, not least, when the older folk of the township were taken into the heart of the communal spirit as manifested by the *ceilidh*. Thus, the *ceilidh* had a definite social function in the crofting township, and was not the occasion for pure entertainment as it tends to be today. The old-time *ceilidh* also served as the present-day community centre does, but was much less formal. The intense social character of such gatherings was fertile ground for the building up of character in the young folk so that they too, in their future time, could make the decisions which would allow them to survive the hardships of the crofting life.

from *Crofting Years* (1984)

Family and Romance

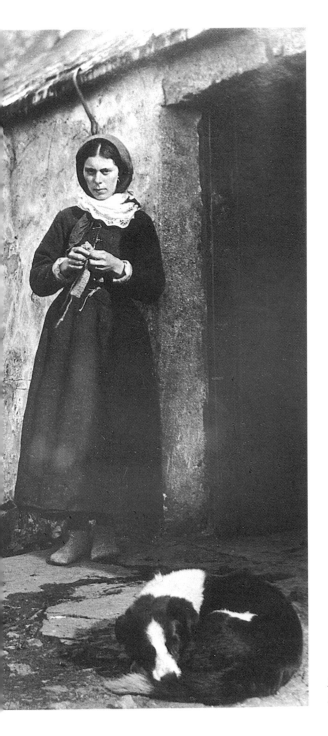

Mrs. Norman MacKinnon,
St. Kilda, 1909.

Òran do Bharbra Nighean Easbuig Fullarton

1.   Thugas gaol nach fàillinneach
     Do ribhinn nan cuach fàmannach,
     Gur bòidheach dualach àr-bhuidhe
       Mar aiteal deàrrsaidh theud.

2.   A' ghruaidh a chruthaich nàdar dhuit,
     Tùs ratha 's rogha dealbha sin,
     'S gach aona buaidh mar a b'fheàrr
       Bh' air Diàna-sa chaidh eug:

3.   Gu maiseach min-gheal tàbhachdach,
     Anns gach gnaoi neo-fhàileasach,
     Aigne sèimh neo-àrdanach,
       Gun fhàillinne fo'n ghréin.

4.   Sùgach an àm mànrain thu,
     Cùirteil mar a b'àbhaist dhi;
     'S math thig faite gàire dhuit
       O chlàragaibh do bhéil.

5.   Gur mils' a pòg na mealannan;
     'S i 's cinntich glòr gun aimideachd –
     Bheir brigh a beòil 's a h-analach
       Neach anacrach o'n eug.

Song to Barbara, Daughter
of Bishop Fullerton

1. I have given unfailing love to the maiden of the waving locks – beautiful, curled and golden yellow, like the shining gleam of harp-strings.

2. The cheek that nature created for you is the prime advantage and the finest of physical beauties; and all the best qualities of Diana, who is long gone:

3. Fair, white and tender, excellent, in every beauty unshadowed; mind gentle and never haughty, without the slightest fault.

4. You are merry in time of festivity, courtly as she always was; well does a smile, with your white teeth, become you.

5. Her kiss is sweeter than honeys, her speech most assured and free from foolishness: the power of her lips and her breath can save those in agony from death.

6.   A h-uchd nach crìon ri thaisbeanadh,
     Bheil dà chìoch cho tlachdmhora
     Bhuin gach cridh' 'na *chaptive* leò
        Fo ghlasaibh aice fhéin.

7.   Is caoin fo gùn a seang-corpan;
     'S i 's maoile glùin is calpannan;
     Troigh bheag chruinn gun gharbhcalachd
        Nach saltair garbh air feur.

8.   Chaidh cliù na té-s' a h-Albainn uainn
     Aig gloinead bheus 's aig leanbanachd:
     Cha d'fhan e anns a' Ghearmailte
        Gun dol gu dearbh do'n Ghréig.

9.   B'fheàrr gur mise bhuaidhicheadh
     Fail le'n cuirteadh cruaidh-shnaim ort:
     Cha b'fhear gun àgh 'san uair sin mi
        Nam buainichinn thu fhéin.

10. Ach 's cruaidh an càs ma's fuatharachd
     Gheibh mi 'n àite truacantachd:
     B'fheàrr dhomh mura buainichinn thu
        Bhith 'san uaigh am péin.

11. Có chuala e no chunnaic e
     No fhuair an nàdar duine e,
     Gach uaisle tha 'm Babaidh Fullarton
     A choinnich ann ad chré?

12. Ge b'e do thoil-sa diùltadh rium,
     Chan onair dhomh bhith diùghaltach:
     Mo shoraidh-sa gu dùrachdach
        Dod' bhrollach cùbhraidh fhéin.

6.   Her bosom so smooth to see, with two breasts so delightful, which have taken all hearts captive, imprisoned by her.

7.   Lovely her slender body in her gown; she has the most perfectly rounded knee and calves; well-rounded little foot devoid of ugliness, which treads gently on the grass.

8.   This lady's fame for purity of manners and childlike qualities has gone from us beyond Scotland: it has not stopped at Germany, but indeed gone on to Greece.

9.   It were best that I should win a ring which would bind you tightly: I would then be no luckless man if I were to win you.

10.   But it is a sorry tale if I am to receive hate rather than compassion: better for me, if I failed to win you, to be suffering in the grave.

11.   Who ever heard it, or saw it, or found it within the nature of man, that all the noble qualities in Babby Fullerton have met in your body?

12.   Though it be your wish to reject me, it is dishonorable for me to be vindictive: farewell sincerely from me to your fragrant breast.

William MacGillivray

Harris

Rose early, took a towel in my pocket, and went over to South town where I washed in the sea. The water felt very cold. Here I observed a flock of ducks, and an immense squadron of scarts passing from their habitacles at the west side of Bencapval to their fishing stations up the sound. The gannet too was fishing. On my way home, I fell in with the cattle, and drank some warm milk – after breakfast I went over to South town in quest of flowers. On returning I prepared for a journey to Scarista, where we were informed there was to be a preaching. Miss Marion accompanied me. Mr Macleod of Marig preached – the sermon was very indifferent – Miss Bethune from Borve and the children, and Duncan McLellan of Ensay, and William McKenzie from Tarbert were all the people of note that I saw. The money collected amounted to thirteen pence halfpenny. Mr Macleod accompanied us to North town. The day was uncommonly fine. After dinner, the ladies and I took a walk to South town, not as people walk in towns but after our own warm highland manner – with my left hand upon Mary's right shoulder, and my right arm about Marion's waist – Our conversation was light and desultory. Miss Marion and I then went to the fold. She has a very good figure and face, but is rather deficient in point of education. She is in short a stout, hale, buxom, highland wench. When we were at tea a gentleman from Uist, Mr Dingwal, came in. I retired soon after, and taking a great coat of Mary's about my shoulders walked solitarily over to the hill of Tashtir. It was about nine of a very fine night – I stood upon an eminence. There was a gentle breeze from the north, the moon shone in a clear skye, thinly sprinkled with stars – the broad line of reflection commencing at the island of Ensay and terminating at Traigh-na-clibhadh showed by the degrees of brightness the different currents in the channel. To the north west the great ocean opened – to the south the sound of Skye. Between these lay, at the distance of some miles the islands Ensay, Berneray and Pabbay, while the hills of Hirta veyed the horizon – The gentle rustling of the corn waving in the breeze, the ripple of the wavelet on the shore, and the scream of the wandering sea bird gave life to the scene. On the other side I had the hills of Harris, those in the distance tipped with gray mist. I recited some pieces of poetry, returned home, and after writing these notes retired to bed about twelve o'clock.

from William MacGillivray's *Journal 1817–1818*

John Grant

Skye

As far as I can remember, the Gaels never placed too much importance in displaying affection to each other, although there was a lot of love between families and between people. You'd only see it very rarely. Particularly if something happened, if something wrong happened, if there was a death, or something. And when families would leave for the mainland, or away overseas. When they'd come back, you'd see it then, but at other times, in normal circumstances, they didn't believe in showing too much affection like that at all. They didn't want to make a 'display' of it, as they say in English. They kept to themselves, but there was love amongst families and amongst friends. They were a bit quiet, and they kept things to themselves.

The men were often away by themselves. And there'd be 'céilidh' houses somewhere, and the men would usually be there in one of those houses. The women wouldn't be together quite so often as the men were. The men would always go out at night, to go céilidhing. And many of the men would gather together there, and there probably wouldn't be any women there at all.

MN: *How did the men choose a woman to marry?*

IG: They very often met in the same village where they were raised. Very few of them used to marry outside the village. Usually they'd always have been familiar with each other, they'd probably have gone to school together, and it was very uncommon for young men in the village to marry girls from somewhere else, when I was young. But after that, when people started travelling, going further afield and working away in other places, that's when they started marrying girls from other places, villages that were some distance away, or even somewhere on

A group, St. Kilda.

A GROUP, ST. KILDA. 6201. G.W.W.

the mainland or one of the Western Isles. And that's how things have continued until this day, it is pretty common.

MN: *Was it because of beauty or some other trait that a male was attracted to a particular female?*

IG: I believe that it was both things, a woman who was pretty and also capable – good at doing things around the house, inside and outside. But in those days, all the women were good at work to be done inside and outside, especially if she was from the same village, or from a small village.

Chrissie Oliver

Eigg

I think it did great damage, to be tearing families apart when the children were at an early age. They'd leave for the mainland at eleven or twelve years of age, and if they kept going to school they wouldn't be at home very often – they'd come home at holidays, and those that left after three years, they would be working on the mainland and going to the cities. I think this breaking up of families is responsible for the terrible amount of oral history and tradition that has been lost – as the children were growing up, they were taken away.

Iain Mac a' Ghobhainn

Do Mo Mhàthair

Bha thus' a' sgoltadh sgadain
ann a Yarmouth fad' air falbh,
's a' ghrian shaillt sa mhadainn
ag èirigh às a' chuan,
's an fhuil air oir do sgine
's an salainn ud cho garbh
's gun thachd e thu o bhruidhinn
's gu robh do bhilean searbh.

Bha mis' an Obar-Dheadhain
a' deoghal cùrsan ùr',
mo Ghàidhlig ann an leabhar
's mo Laideann aig an stiùir,
'nam shuidh' an siud air cathair
's mo chofaidh ri mo thaobh
is duilleagan a' crathadh
siùil na sgoilearachd 's mo thùir.

The cionta ga mo lèireadh
mar a dh'èirich 's mar a tha.
Cha bu chaomh leam a bhith 'g èirigh
ann an doilleireachd an là,
bhith a' sgoltadh 's a bhith reubadh
iasg na maidne air an tràigh,
's am muir borb ud a bhith beucadh

sìos mo mhiotagan gun tàmh.

Ged a nì mi sin 'nam bhàrdachd,
's e m'fhuil fhìn a th' air mo làimh,
's gach aon sgadan thug an làn dhomh
a' plosgartaich gu 'n dèan mi dàn,
's an àite cùbair tha mo chànan
cruaidh is teann orm a ghnàth
is an salainn garbh air m'fhàinne
a' toirt beòthalachd don bhàs.

To My Mother

Iain Crichton Smith

You were gutting herring in distant Yarmouth, and the salt sun in the morning rising out of the sea, the blood on the edge of your knife, and that salt so coarse that it stopped you from speaking and made your lips bitter.

I was in Aberdeen sucking new courses, my Gaelic in a book and my Latin at the tiller, sitting there on a chair with my coffee beside me and leaves shaking the sails of scholarship and my intelligence.

Guilt is tormenting me because of what happened and how things are. I would not like to be getting up in the darkness of the day gutting and tearing the fish of the morning on the shore and that savage sea to be roaring down my gloves without cease.

Though I do that in my poetry, it is my own blood that is on my hands, and every herring that the high tide gave me palpitating till I make a song, and instead of a cooper my language always hard and strict on me, and the coarse salt on my ring bringing animation to death.

Peigi Stewart

Skye

My father was really very good with children. He used to sit us on his knee and sing to us, the knee used to be going anywhere and we really used to be shoogled up and down. Oh, he had such a lot of patience, my father. Yes, he used to play games with us. We might be out herding the cows and, you know, keeping his eye on the cows, he would come out. And if we had a ball he would join us and play ball with us. Or he used to race with the boys, you know, race to see who was the fastest from one point to another.

He's an old seaman, and he had a fishing boat at that time and he would show us how to tie the different knots and we also had to mend the nets sometimes.

He had practically all the Gilleasbuig Aotrom stories, and he used to tell them to us. Or maybe there was somebody in and something would have happened and one of those stories would come to his mind and he would tell it. Like the time he [Gilleasbuig] was in Portree and he was down in the fishing ports and somebody had given him a cod. And he thought, 'Well, I must make some money on this cod!' And he went to a house and said to them, 'Now I've got a nice cod here, would you like to buy it?' It would all be in Gaelic, of course. And for a shilling. So the woman of the house would say, 'Oh, yes, I'll have the cod.' And he would say, 'Well, I'll just go and clean it myself for you myself.' And instead of going and cleaning it, of course, he would go on to the next house and he would do the same thing in every house and make himself quite a few shilling. I've heard my father telling that story. And lots of other Gilleasbuig Aotrom stories he had.

We didn't have any toys, what they call toys nowadays and people spend fortunes on. But we were just as happy. We used to find things to do. We used to get catalogues and cut out all the ladies and then we used to have shops. We used to have to invent everything we did overselves.

You'd play some terrible pranks on Halloween. Even the boys when I was going to school, they used to play some terrible pranks on people. I don't know that they would dress up. But you see it would be dark and they would, maybe somebody's cart was lying in their field and they would, you know, shift it to an entirely different place. Things like that. I believe lots of them used to pinch the cabbages too. Pinch turnips.

Finlay J MacDonald

Harris

Like all the women on the distaff side of my father's family, Great Aunt Rachel was built like a Churchill tank with a personality to match. She was also literate in that she could write and read English, which was not all that usual in her generation in our part of the world. And that, in itself, was enough to set her apart. She claimed to have met Lord macaulay, which seemed to make a huge impression on people even though they had never heard of the great writer, and she could produce two crystal goblets which he had given her. All of which would seem to be perfectly feasible since the said Lord Macaulay's great grandfather had been minister of her old parish (the one we were about to enter into) and that reverend gentleman had carved himself a niche in eighteenth-century history by being the only man who tried to betray Bonnie Prince Charlie when the latter was being hunted in the Western Isles after Culloden. That particular bit of the story seemed to have escaped Aunt Rachel's capacious memory!

Mary MacDonald,
South Uist.

The crystal goblets were strictly for display and were only brought out to be polished or to be exhibited to some special visitor. They couldn't possibly be of any more practical use anyway in an environment as morally and economically stringent as hers, and they would have looked absurd with the thick black tea to which she was so thoroughly addicted.

No ancient or modern brewer of real ale was more devoted to his tipple than Aunt Rachel was to her tea. And no alchemist took greater care with the blending of his potions. She never used a teapot. She used a little black pan which she filled to within an inch of the top with fresh spring water and placed on the open fire so that it could absorb the flavour of the peat smoke that curled up around it as it came to the boil. When it began to bubble she added half a fistful of tea from a large caddy sporting a fading picture of Queen Victoria, whom, come to think of it, she resembled in more ways than one, and the brew was made to boil vigorously while she knitted a measured knuckle of sock which she had calculated long ago took her ten minutes. The fact that she got arthritic and slower as she got older didn't alter anything. As far as she was concerned an inch and a half of sock was still ten minutes, and that was the duration for which tea boiled. The tea got blacker as Great Aunt Rachel's hair got whiter, and she lived to be very old. Latterly her fainter-hearted visitors used to conjure up all sorts of excuses to get out of having to partake of her hospitality, and it was useless for her sister or her stepdaughter, who guessed at the reason for the reluctance, to suggest a milder distillation. But it was only well behind her back that anybody dared smile at the old lady's oft-quoted assertion – in which the pun evaded her innocence in both her languages – 'When I make tea I make tea, and when I make water I make water.'

from *Crowdie and Cream* (1982)

Norman MacCaig

Aunt Julia

Aunt Julia spoke Gaelic
very loud and very fast.
I could not answer her—
I could not understand her.

She wore men's boots
when she wore any.
—I can see her strong foot,
stained with peat,
paddling with the treadle of the spinningwheel
while her right hand drew yarn
marvellously out of the air.

Hers was the only house
where I've lain at night
in the absolute darkness
of a box bed, listening to
crickets being friendly.

She was buckets
and water flouncing into them.
She was winds pouring wetly
round house-ends.
She was brown eggs, black skirts
and a keeper of threepennybits
in a teapot.

Aunt Julia spoke Gaelic
very loud and very fast.
By the time I had learned
a little, she lay
silenced in the absolute black
of a sandy grave
at Luskentyre.
But I hear her still, welcoming me
with a seagull's voice
across a hundred yards
of peatscrapes and lazybeds
and getting angry, getting angry
with so many questions unanswered.

Mrs. Janet MacIntyre, Eriskay, 1934.

Kate Dix

Berneray
The Fairy Suitor Foiled

There was a house at Bornish in South Uist, and it was just a little thatched house, but many a one called there. Every house at that time had a partition in it. And they killed their cow when it grew old. And they used to dry the hide to make garments and boots and all sorts of things out of it, even laces: they made laces for their shoes. And the cow's hide was hung over the partition.

And there was one girl in the house with her father and mother. And the girl was very beautiful, and she used to go to the hill with the cattle every day and come back in, and go out again in the evening and bring them home. And there was a man who used to meet her in the hill, a bonny lad – she had never seen anyone so handsome as him. And he would walk with her till she was nearly home, and he left, and came back, and it went on like that for six months. She used to wonder – for she was deeply in love with the lad – why he never said a word to her, and how nobody had ever seen him before. She asked everyone, but they had never seen or heard of such a man at all.

She went to a kind old tinker woman who lived down there, and she told her the whole story.

'Oh, my dear,' said she, 'when you go home, take a strand from the tail of the cowhide hanging on the partition, and wash and clean it and make it up into a bonny plait, and lay it aside. And before long that lad will ask for a lock of your hair. And when he asks for a lock of your hair you must go and give him the plait you got from the cow's tail.'

As the poor old woman said, that's how it happened. It wasn't long before the lad asked her for a lock of her hair, and she said, 'I'll bring it for you tonight when I go for the cattle.' And she did that.

And when they were holding family worship at midnight, the hide over the partition began to hop. It began to hop, and jump, and hop like mad. They leapt to open the door, and out went the skin. They went after it, everyone who was around, with dogs and men and horses. They couldn't catch it or keep up with it until it reached the knoll they called Cnoc an t-Sidhein [the Fairy Knoll]. It stopped there and it went and vanished from sight, and they never found the hide again.

And they said that if the girl had given him her own hair, she would havre gone and she would never have come back again. That's what I heard.

Recorded and translated from Gaelic (1968)

Clearances
and Exile

*SS Hebrides lying
in Village Bay, St. Kilda.*

The Clearances refer to the period roughly stretching from the 1790s to the 1850s when large numbers of the population in the Highlands and Islands were cleared by landlords from the land to make way for firstly sheep farming and then deer forests. Many were moved to less fertile land on the coast of Scotland and the islands and abroad to the New World. There was great strength of feeling about the clearances as the oral histories and songs which follow make clear. There is still however controversy over the consequences of the clearances, about land use and the role of landlords, and about the economic development of the Highlands and Islands.

Professor Geikie

Skye

'One of the most vivid recollections I retain of Kilbride is that of the eviction, or the clearance of the crofters of Suisnish. The corner of Strath between the two sea-inlets of Lochs Slapin and Eishort had been for ages occupied by a community that cultivated the Lower ground, where their huts formed a kind of scattered village. The land belonged to the wide domain of Lord Macdonald, whose affairs were in such a state that he had to place himself in the hands of trustees. These men had little local knowledge of the estate; and though they doubtless administered it to the best of their ability, their main object was to make as much money as possible out of the rents, so as, on the one hand, to satisfy the creditors, and, on the other, to hasten the time when the proprietor might be able to resume possession. The interests of the crofters formed a very secondary consideration. With these aims, the trustees determined to clear out the whole population of Suisnish and convert the ground into one large sheep farm, to be placed in the hands of a responsible grazier, if possible from the south country.'

'I had heard some rumours of these intentions, but did not realise they were in process of being carried into effect until one afternoon, as I was returning from my ramble, a strange wailing sound reached my ears at intervals on the breeze from the west. On gaining the top of a hill on the south side of the valley, I could see a long and motley procession wending along the road that led from Suisnish. It halted at the point in the road opposite Kilbride, and there the lamentation became long and loud.'

'As I drew nearer, I could see that the minister, with his wife and daughters, had come out to meet the people and bid them all farewell. It was a miscellaneous gathering of at least three generations of crofters. There were old men and women, too feeble to walk, who were placed in carts, the younger members of the community on foot were carrying their bundles of clothes and household effects, while the children, with looks of alarm, walked alongside.'

'There was a pause in the notes of woe as the last words were exchanged with the family of Kilbride. Every one was in tears; each wished to clasp the hands that had so often befriended them; and it seemed as if they could not tear themselves away. When they set off once more, a cry of grief went up to heaven; the long plaintive wail, like a funeral coronach, was resumed; and, after the last of the emigrants had disappeared behind the hill, the sound seemed to re-echo through the whole wide valley of Strath in one prolonged note of desolation. The people were on their way to be shipped to Canada. I have often wandered since then over the solitary ground of Suisnish. Not a soul is to be seen there now.

quoted in *History of Skye* (1930)

Photograph of Emigrants

Iain Crichton Smith
Lewis

Your faces cheerful though impoverished,
you stand at the rail, tall-collared and flat-capped.
You are leaving Lewis (Stornoway) behind.
Before you the appalling woods will rise
after the sea's sharp salt, your axes hack
the towering trunks. What are you leaving now? –
The calm routine of winding chimney smoke,
the settled village with its small sparse fields,
the ceilidhs and the narratives. Deceived
by chiefs and lairds, by golden promises,
you set off, smiling towards a new world,
Canada with its Douglas firs and snow,
its miles of desolate emptiness.

               Why do I weep
to see these faces, thin and obsolete,
these Sunday ties and collars, by the rail,
as the ship moves, and you move with it,
towards your flagrant destinies of sharp
bony starvation, ruinous alcohol.
All shall be revealed but at this time
your faces blaze with earnestness, and joy,
as if you were coming home instead of leaving.
Nothing will save some standing by the rail.

others will come home in tartan caps,
a fury of possessions, and a love
of what's disappeared forever when they left,
themselves not being able to be there and here,
and therefore growing differently towards pictures
which frame them where they stand, thus staring out
into the inscrutable waters of their fates.

Dean Cadalan Samhach, A Chuilean Mo Ruin

Dean cadalan sàmhach, a chuilean mo rùin;
Dean fuireach mar tha thu, 's tu an dràsd' an àit' ùr.
Bidh òigearan againn, làn beairteis 'us cliù,
'S ma bhios tu 'nad airidh, 's leat fear-eiginn dhiubh.

Gur ann an America tha sinn an dràsd',
Fo dhubhar na coille, nach teirig gu bràth.
'N uair dh'fhalbhas an dùlachd 's a thionndaidh's am blàths,
Bithidh cnothan, bidh ùbhlan 's bithidh an siùcar a'fàs.

'S ro bheag orm féin na daoine seo th'ann,
Le 'n còtaichean drògaid, ad mhór air an ceann;
Le 'm briogaisean goirid, 's iad sgaoilte gu 'm bonn;
Chan fhaicear an to-osan, 's i' bhochdainn a th'ann.

Tha sinne 'n ar n-Innseanaich, cinnteach gu leòir;
Fo dhubhar nan craobh, cha bhi h-aon againn beò;
Madaidh alluidh 'us béistean ag éigheach 's gach fròig;
Gu bheil sinne 'nar n-éiginn bho'n là thréig sinn Righ Deòrs'.

Thoir mo shoraidh le fàilte Chinn t-Sàile nam bó,
Far 'n d'fhuair mi greis m' àrach 's mi'm phàisde beag òg.
Bhiodh fleasgaichean donn air bonnaibh ri ceòl,
Agus nionagan dualach 's an gruaidh mar an ròs.

An toiseach an fhoghair bu chridheil ar sunnd,
Am fiadh anns an fhireach, 's am bradan an grunnd;
Bhiodh luingeas an sgadain a' tighinn fo shiùil;
Bu bhòidheach a' sealladh 's fir dhonn air am bùird.

Sleep Softly, My Darling Beloved

Sleep softly, my darling beloved.
Stay as you are, now that you are in a new land.
We'll find suitors abounding in wealth and fame,
and, if you are worthy, you shall have one of them.

We are now in America,
in the shade of the never-ending forest.
When winter departs and warmth returns,
nuts, apples, and sugar will grow.

Little do I like the people who are here,
with their drugget coats, tall hats on their heads,
and their short breeches split to the ends.
Hose are never seen, and that is a pity.

We've become Indians surely enough.
Skulking under trees, not one of us will be left alive,
with wolves and beasts howling in every lair.
We've come to ruin since the day we forsook King George.

Bear my farewell and greeting to Kintail and its cattle,
where I spent my time of upbringing when I was a young child.
There dark-haired lads would dance heel and toe to the music,
and lassies with flowing tresses and cheeks like the rose.

At the onset of harvest-time our spirits would be joyous;
deer on the moors and salmon in the pools;
the herring fleet would come in under sail;
a fine sight with brown-haired lads on board.

Empty house,
Waterloo, Skye.

Women in the front line

Joni Buchanan

Sollas in North Uist deserves an honoured place in the history of crofter resistance. The form it took, in response to evictions in 1849, followed a pattern of protest already established as early as the 1820s at Culrain and Gruids; later also at Glencalvie and Coigach. It put women in the vanguard of protest.

In the first days of August 1849, Lord MacDonald set about clearing between 400–500 people from his North Uist estate. A young reporter from the 'Inverness Courier' accompanied the eviction party and has left us a meticulous account of the event which I recently came across.

Earlier in the year, when sheriff officers had attempted to evict the Sollas people they were deforced, and sent on their way. For their second attempt, they came prepared. Thirty-three police constables were drafted in from Inverness under the charge of Mr MacBean, Superintendent of the County Police.

The Established Church minister, Rev MacRae, was also on board the steamer as it set off to Lochmaddy. It stopped at Armadale to let MacDonald know they were ready to proceed and also to 'receive any suggestions his Lordship might make to the betterment of conditions there'. But Lord MacDonald had no suggestions.

The Rev MacRae, after a lengthy interview, was also unable to 'obtain any modifications of his views'. The party headed for Lochmaddy, where they were joined early the following morning by Mr Patrick Cooper, MacDonald's Commissioner. He had travelled by mail packet overnight from Dunvegan.

'He immediately expressed his intentions to proceed with the ejectment of the whole of the population in the district of Sollas – unless previous offers of emigration made to the people were agreed to,' reported the 'Courier'.

By that he meant the entire population of the four farm towns of Sollas, Dunskeller, Middlequarter and Mallaglate.

At Mid-day, the police arrived at the brow of the hill overlooking the townships. The minute they were spotted, three signals were raised from one of the houses, and 'people from all the neighbourhood were seen crowding along the paths leading to the house from which the signals were flying, and around which a large crowd of men women and children had already assembled'.

Cooper tried to forestall resistance by proclaiming it was still not too late to accept the 'offer' of emigration. Four or five families conceded defeat and agreed to emigrate.

It was too late in the day to proceed with evictions. Instead the party decided to arrest those men who had previously deforced the sheriff officers. Roderick MacLean and Angus MacPhail were handcuffed and marched off to Lochmaddy.

At this a large group of women 'raised a continued yell and seizing stones rushed down the hill to intercept the march'. After a while they were calmed by the minister and MacBean.

On the Thursday morning when the evicting party arrived to continue their dirty work, not a soul was to be seen. In the last desperate attempt to protect their families and pitiful belongings they stayed indoors, but that did not hinder MacDonald's henchmen.

When the first tenant, by the name of MacPherson was asked to emigrate, he refused – and in two or three minutes the few articles of furniture he possessed were turned out the door and his house left roofless.

The wife of the prisoner Angus MacPhail was among the next to be ejected. The 'Courier' correspondent wrote: 'Her domestic plenishings were of the simplist character – its greatest, and by far its most valuable part being three small children.' The woman was half-clad and her face swollen from crying: she was placed on the poor roll, but was also ejected.

The sheriff, who must have been a man of some humanity, refused to evict

Dun Carloway,
Lewis.

the next eight families – some were old, and others too poor to be turned out. But Cooper was anxious that they should all be removed elsewhere. It must have been a pitiful scene.

from *The West Highland Free Press*

Nan MacKinnon

Vatersay

When the Gordons came to Barra and were turning people out of their houses, my grandfather was a ground-officer. And they had a policeman from Skye in Barra too. And they had both given an undertaking – my grandfather and the policeman – to make holes in the houses over the heads of the people and put out their fires. The Skye policeman and my grandfather didn't want to do this, but they had to do it to save their own skins. And the Skye policeman and my grandfather used to go round the houses, and the Skye policeman had a stick, and he would shove it through a divot and through the hatch and he would say to my grandfather, 'Is that not holed, Finlay?'

'Yes,' said my grandfather, 'we'll know what we mean, lad,' he would say.

They had given their word, but for all that it went against the grain for them to do what they were supposed to do. But they would make holes in the houses with the stick, and they would go in and throw a bucket of water on the fire and put it out. And when they had gone away again the people would stop up this hole that they had made in the thatch. They would kindle the fire again. But all the same when they went back to the Gordons they would have to say that they had made holes in the houses over their head and put out their fires.

But many left Barra because of this. They were put out against their will, and some left in MacNeil's time too ... Some of them were willing enough to leave in a way, for, poor souls, they had no land. They had nothing but the bare rocks, and ... the people who owned Barra, the landlords, as they would say themselves, they were so hard on them. They had two rents to pay. They had to hand over a pailful of seed corn along with the rent, and it's over in Nask, that's where they used to pay the rent, and the place is called Tobhta an Dà Mhàil [the ruin of the two rents] to this day.

from *Tocher* vol. 3, no. 17

Language
and
Island Life

Neil Gillies sending
off mailboat from St. Kilda, 1938.

Ceud Bliadhna Sa Sgoil

Ruaraidh MacThòmais

Ceud bliadhna sa sgoil
is sinn nar Gaidheil fhathast!
Cò shaoileadh gum biodh an fhreumh cho righinn?
Dhòirt iad eallach leabhraichean oirnn,
is cànanan, eachdraidh choimheach,
is saidheans, is chuir iad maidse riutha.
O abair lasair
de mhinistearan 's de mhaighstirean-sgoile,
de dhoctairean 's de dh'einnsinidhears,
profeasairean is luchd-reic-chàraichean,
ach aig ceann nan ceud blianna,
an dèidh gach greadain 's gach dadhaidh,
nuair a sguab iad an luath air falbh,
bha a fhreumh ann a sin fhathast,
fann-bhuidhe an toiseach.
Is minig a chunna sinn craobh a chaidh a losgadh –
A! 'sann le fun tha mi,
na biodh eagal oirbh a luchd-stiùiridh an fhoghlaim,
a chomhairlichean na siorrachd, is a' Bheurla cho math agaibh –
a' fàs –
siud sibh, sguabaibh a' chlann a Steòrnabhagh –
nas braise.

A Hundred Years in School

Derick Thomson
Lewis

A hundred years in school
and we're Gaels still!
Who would have thought the root was so tough?
They poured a load of books on us,
languages, foreign history,
science, and put a match to them.
O what a blaze
of ministers and dominies,
doctors and engineers,
professors and car-salesmen,
but after a hundred years,
after each scorching and singeing,
when they brushed away the ash
the root was there still,
pale-yellow at first.
We have often seen a bush that was burnt –
I'm just joking,
have no fear, directors of education,
county councillors, with your fluent English –
growing –
that's right, centralise education in Stornoway –
faster.
Ceud Bliadhna Sa Sgoil

Tir A'Mhurain,
South Uist, 1954.

Ar Cànan 's ar Clò

Anne Frater
Lewis

Bha bodach na mo bhaile
aig an robh beairt,
agus leis a' bheairt
dhèanadh e clò,
agus chaidh aodach
a dhèanamh den chlò,
agus bhiodh na daoine
a' cur orra 'n aodaich –
aodach tiugh trom a chumadh blàth iad.
Ach thàinig fear eile,
fear na b'òige,
fear nach buineadh don bhaile,
agus bha beairt ùr aige
agus snàth ùr –
dathan air an goid bhon bhogha-froise –
agus aodach tana, lom,
agus àlainn, ann am beachd nan daoine.
Chum am bodach air
leis an t-seann bheairt
ach bha na daoine òg
a' fanaid air,
agus cheannaich iad uile
nan beairtean ùra,
agus thòisich iad a' dèanamh

Our Tongue and Our Tweed

Anne Frater
Lewis

There was an old man in my village
who had a loom,
and with his loom
he would make tweed,
and clothes were made
from the tweed,
and the people
would wear the clothes –
thick, heavy clothes that would keep them warm.
But another man came,
a younger man,
one who was not a native of the village,
and he had a new loom
and new yarn –
colours stolen from the rainbow –
and thin, smooth cloth
which the people found beautiful.
The old man carried on
with the old loom
but the young folk
laughed at him,
and they all bought
the new looms,
and they began to make

nan clòitean ùra,
agus cha robh dragh aca
mu dheidhinn a' chlò
air beairt a' bhodaich.
Ach, an dèidh ùine
thàinig an geamhradh
agus cha chumadh an t-aodach lom
le na snàithtean brèagha
agus na dathan soilleir
a-mach am fuachd,
agus cha robh feum
anns na beairtean ùra.
Lorg iad am bodach
agus chunnaic iad a' bheairt,
agus chunnaic iad an clò,
ach cha b'urrainn dhaibh
a' bheairt obrachadh,
oir bha i air fàs meirgeach
agus bha am bodach marbh.

the new cloth,
and they did not care
for the tweed
on the old man's loom.
But, after a while,
winter came
and the smooth cloth
with the lovely threads
and the bright colours
could not keep out the cold,
and the new looms
were useless.
They sought the old man
and they saw his loom,
and they saw the tweed,
and they were unable
to work the loom
because it had rusted
and the old man was dead.

Iain Crichton Smith

Lewis

It is not a witticism to say 'Shall Gaelic die?' What that means is 'Shall we die?' For on the day that I go home to the island and speak to my neighbour in English it is not only the language that has died but in a sense the two who no longer speak it. We would be elegies on the face of the earth, empty and without substance. We would not represent anything, and the world would be an orphan about us.

I imagine those who lose their language dying in the same way as the language dies, spiritless, without pride. One imagines the tourist then entering a world which would truly be inferior to his own. One imagines the beggars of the spirit, no longer real people in a real place. They will be shadows cast by an imperialistic language that is not their own. For if they speak a language that is not their own they are slaves in the very centre of themselves. They will have been colonised completely at the centre of the spirit, they will be dead, exiles, not abroad but in their own land, which will not reflect back the names they have given it. Such a people will be a race of shadows and in that final silence there will be no creativity. They will be superfluous, talking without alternative in a language that is not their own.

from *Towards the Human* (1986)

Willie MacKinnon

Mull

The way of life in the islands is getting different. It's not the way it was a few years ago because you've got a big influx of English now. Very big influx of English into the islands. They used to look at us with scorn, you know. And there was always the myth of the Hielan' man running around with a ragged kilt, in the heather, swinging a claymore and chasing a haggis. This is what they thought at first. But they realise now that life in the islands is a damn sight better than what they can get in the cities – with the result that a lot of people reckon that it's the Highland clearances in a different way. They are forcing their way of life onto us. You've got to conform more to the English way of life, not the Scottish way of life. They get themselves elected onto different things. They elect themselves into the upper echelons and then what they say goes. A lot of businesses on the island are owned by English people. Before very long there won't be a Mac left in these parts.

from *Island Voices* (1992)

Kate Ann MacLellan

North Uist

We all talk Gaelic in the home. My sons were brought up in the Gaelic and it's Gaelic they talk all the time, and they prefer it to English.

When I was going to school, it was all Gaelic in the playground. You never heard an English word spoken. Children who were Gaelic speakers would be just kind of looked down on if they started speaking in English. But then, of course, incomers started coming in and that meant that when their children went to school, it wasn't so easy for the local children because they were hearing English in the playground and I think quite a lot of them were taken by it. I think they preferred to be speaking English, the same as the incomers were.

So, gradually, in the local community you would hardly hear any of the children speaking Gaelic. And now, in quite a lot of houses where there are children, I hear the mother and father speaking English to them instead of the Gaelic, and I don't believe in that at all.

from *Island Voices* (1992)

Croft,
Bornish, South Uist.

Angus Peter Campbell

South Uist

More peat carrying. I now understand why the Gaelic heartland is dying; too long a sacrifice can make a stone of the heart. After generations of grinding labour, if electricity and running water and coal and cars and TV came along, would you not also grab at them with both wild hands? The real imperialist triumph was that, meantime, Gaelic became psychologically associated with the grinding labour part whilst English was the currency of the other polished world where electricity arrived miraculously, where sparkling water poured from a tap, where shining coal arrived in sacks, where gleaming cars sat at the doors and where the TV amazed us with marvellous images of mighty elephants traversing across the oh-so-green African parks. Is it any wonder that we bought the linguistic lie along with everything else?

Meantime, a whole generation of learners attend a Gaelic college, where I teach, to learn the language. Is it any wonder that native speakers, who feel they have borne the physical and psychological burdens long enough, are sceptical of a new generation which acquires the language in a windswept coastal village? This, of course, is the very issue that divides the Old from the New Testament; law and grace. How were God's chosen people, honed over persecuted centuries, expected to accept that salvation was now freely and instantly available to anyone, thanks to Christ's death on the cross? It's still hard to accept, because we all enjoy watching people carrying sacks.

Walking through the wet bog, sack on back, I just want to fling it off. I do, and the relief is wonderful.

Extract from a diary from *The Scottish Review* (1996)

Iain Crichton Smith

Lewis

In a society which is still concerned with class to a great extent, it is important to say that the community in which I grew up was a classless one. It is possible that, seen from the outside, the islanders might be characterised as belonging to a peasant society. Seen from the inside, however, the islander does not think of himself as a peasant nor does he consider himself as being set in a particular social scale. Indeed questions of that nature have never really troubled him, and when I myself first read the works of the Angry Young Men – and especially those of Osborne – I did not feel that this had any meaning for me. It was later, when I first encountered some of the members of what may be called the English Southern Belt, that I recognised class at all, and was shocked by it, for to believe that a man or woman can be labelled according to income and school seems to me an abomination of the human spirit.

It is true that the islander looked up to the schoolmaster and the minister and indeed, certainly in the past, would cut the minister's peats without taking payment. But the reason why they looked up to these men had nothing to do with class. It was a recognition of their usefulness to the community. Education in particular was respected, not as a method of climbing out of one's class but, to a far greater extent than is common nowadays, for its own sake.

from *Towards the Human* (1986)

Customs
and Beliefs

Roadside shrine to the
Virgin Mary, South Uist.

Adomnan of Iona

How the saint spoke with foresight about a great whale

One day, while the blessed man was living in Iona, a brother called Berach, who was on the point of sailing for Tiree, came to St Columba in the morning for a blessing. The saint looked at him closely and said:

'My son, you must be very careful today. Do not try to go directly across the open sea to Tiree, but instead take the roundabout route by the Treshnish Islands. Otherwise you may be terrified by a monster of the deep and find yourself scarcely able to escape.'

With the saint's blessing he set off and boarded his boat, but he went against the saint's advice as though he thought little of it. While crossing the open sea between Iona and Tiree he and those with him in the boat saw – look! – a whale of extraordinary size, which rose up like a mountain above the water, its jaws open to show an array of teeth. At once the men dropped the sail and took to the oars, turning back in terror, but they only just managed to avoid the wash caused by the whale's motion. Remembering what the saint had foretold, they were filled with awe.

That same morning Baithéne was also going to sail to Tiree. The saint said to him:

'In the middle of last night, a great whale rose up from the depths of the sea, and today it will heave itself up on the surface of the sea between Iona and Tiree.'

Baithéne answered him:

'That beast and I are both in God's power.'

'Go in peace,' said the saint. 'Your faith in Christ will shield you from this danger.'

Baithéne was blessed by the saint and set sail from the harbour. They had already crossed a considerable stretch of sea when Baithéne and those with him saw the whale. While all his companions were terrified, Baithéne without a tremor of fear raised his hands and blessed the sea and the whale. Immediately, the great creature plunged under the waves and was not seen again.

from *Life of St Columba*; translated by Richard Sharpe

Mrs Christina Shaw

Harris

CS: On Monday night there would be the *rèiteach* and the marriage would be on the Tuesday, usually, and there would be a wedding celebration that night, and there would be a *banais-taighe* ('house-wedding' or infare) in the man's house then on the Wednesday night. We sometimes stayed up for three nights without going to sleep at all.

PM: Yes. Well, when one of my sisters married, there were four occasions, the small *rèiteach*, the big *rèiteach*, the wedding in our own house and the wedding in his house. There were the four . . .

MM: Now, what happened at the small rèiteach?

PM: Oh, there was nothing but just a sort of party. Only a few people would be there for the small *rèiteach*. And the big *rèiteach* now – they used to decide on the night – the day on which the marriage was to be. And usually it was a week from when it would be – say it was on a Thursday, a week the following Tuesday would be the wedding . . . And the big *rèiteach*, it was just as – just as many people at it, and as much music and food and everything as there was at weddings.

MM: Do you remember any of the things they did at the big *rèiteach*?

CS: Two or three were selected, of the boys who were in – yes, and old men

– to go amongst the girls, grabbing one here and one there and dragging her along to the top of the table, and sometimes manhandling her. And we used to hide, from shyness, in case we were taken up to the groom. And they would appear in the doorway with this one and that one, asking, 'Is this her?'

'Oh no. No. That one's too difficult to winter.'

And one was so ugly, one so fat, one was too thin, and everything was wrong – each one had a fault. And they took old women up too. It didn't matter who they came across, and a lot of the girls hid and went out to the byres in case they were caught. But at last, now, the right one was got hold of, and she would be taken up to the top of the table and seated next to the man. And the man who was asking for the young woman would say, 'Oh, here she is, here she is. We'll accept that one.' That's how they were. 'That one will do.'

MM: And was a drink taken then? Was a dram . . .

CS: Yes. Oh, gracious, by the bottleful, kept going among the people in the seats and chairs.

from *Tocher* 30

Canon Angus MacQueen

South Uist

As Hebridean Christians you met everything head-on. I remember when I was four or five a neighbour died – an old man I loved very much. I used to sit on his knee at the end of the house and he used to tell me about *Tir nan Og*, all those lovely tales. And he died and my father took me so that I would touch his forehead and feel the touch of death so that I would never be afraid of death again.

I was amazed when I met someone recently – a city person – who just couldn't face death because they had never touched or had hardly seen a dead person. They were going into their forties and they just couldn't take death. Whereas things like death and suffering weren't hidden from us. They didn't hide people who were in pain and suffering. One went to sit with them and visit them and listen to them moaning and groaning. And one knew death from a very early age. You knew what was best in life and you knew what one had to put up with. I remember longing for that old man because he was such a lovely old man and I thought my heart would break when he died and I realised he wasn't going to come back.

from *Island Voices* (1992)

Martin Martin

It was an antient Custom in the Islands, that a Man should take a Maid to his Wife, and keep her the space of a Year without marrying her; and if she pleased him all the while, he marry'd her at the end of the Year, and legitimated these Children: but if he did not love her, he return'd her to her Parents, and her Portion also; and if there happen'd to be any Children, they were kept by the Father: but this unreasonable Custom was long ago brought in disuse.

from *A Description of the Western Islands of Scotland* (c. 1695)

Alexander Nicholson

Skye

The two betrothals were still observed – '*an reiteach beag*', when the parties became engaged and '*an reiteach mór*', when a final settlement was made as to the amount of dowry to be given, and other particulars. The '*tocher*' usually consisted of so many cows, the number varying from two to twenty, or even more, according to the substance of the donor.

The ceremony of betrothal, usually attended with much hilarity, and not a little bickering was often indulged in as the parents or the guardians of the contracting parties haggled over the amount of the marriage portion. These cavillings often developed into bitter recriminations, when old sores were re-opened and fierce fights in consequence ensued.

On the morning of the wedding-day people gathered from wide areas, and the custom still prevailed whereby the guests were expected to bring their own provisions. The friends of the bride met in her home, those of the groom in his, and they were entertained separately. After the wedding the parties joined. The duration of the festivity depended on the amount of the commissariat, such functions being carried on sometimes for as long as three days.

On the first morning after the marriage, the bride's mother, or, failing her, the groom's, entered the bed-chamber and bound the bride's hair in the '*breid beannach*', the pointed linen coif, before she left her bed. When the bride arose, she was dressed by the young ladies present and on the completion of her toilet a procession was formed, and her attendants marched out of the chamber led by the bride herself. The first man to accost her on leaving the room was obliged to address her in verse, the greeting being termed, '*Beannachadh Bàird*', or the 'Poet's Blessing'. This custom was honoured with strict insistence and few would care to shun the obligation. It is related by the 'Clans' Historian',

Alexander Mackenzie, that on the occasion of the marriage of the Rev. Donald MacLeod of Duirinish, who afterwards became the third laird of Greshornish, poetic inspiration so failed the guests that none was prepared to offer the bride the customary salutation. As none would venture, and the young bride's arrival was due, the duty of performing the time-honoured ceremony devolved on the bridegroom himself; and his composition, though somewhat lengthy, is worthy of being quoted, owing to the beauty of its sentiment and its lofty moral tone:

'Mìle fàilte dhuit led' bhréid;
Fad' do ré gun robh thu slàn.
Móran làithean dhut le sìth,
Led' mhaitheas, is le d' ni bhi fàs.

A' chulaidh cheutach a chaidh suas
'S tric a tharruing buaidh air mnaoi;
Bi-sa subhailceach, ceutach,
A thionnsgain thu féin 's an stri.

An tùs do còmhraidh is tu òg,
An tùs gach lò iarr Dia nan Dùl;
'S chan eagal nach dean thu gu ceart

Gach dearbh bheachd a bhios 'nad rùn.

Bi-sa fialaidh, ach bi glic,
Bi misneachail, ach bi stòld.
Na bi bruidhneach, 's na bi bàlbh,
Na bi mear, no marbh, 's tu òg.

Bi gleidhteach air do dheagh rùn:
Ach na bi dùinte, 's na bi fuar,
Na labhair air neach gu h-olc,
'S ged labhrar ort, na taisbein fuath.

Na bi gearanach fo chrois;
Falbh socrach le cupan làn.
Chaoidh do'n olc na tabhair spéis,
'S le do bhréid ort – mìle fàilt.'

'A thousand welcomes to you in your coif;
May health be yours throughout your life
With many days in peace,
And, in your goodness, growth in your means.

The splendid headdress you have donned
Has often brought prosperity to a wife;
Be thou virtuous and pleasing,
On entering upon your trial.

At the beginning of your talk in your youth,
And in the morning of your day, seek thy God;
And there will be no fear but you will do the right
In each resolve in your regard.

Be generous but be wise,
Be courageous but be calm.,
Be not talkative but be not dumb
Be not wanton or vapid when young.

Be guarded about your good intentions;
But be not silent or cold,
Speak no ill of any one,
And though you be vilified show no anger.

Complain not of difficulties
Move steadily with a full cup.
Never show favour to wickedness,
And with your coif a thousand welcomes.'

from *History of Skye* (1930)

Religion

It is hard to travel far in the Hebrides, and even more difficult to understand them, without at least trying to get to grips with the religious cultures and influences. Many visitors bring their backgrounds, misunderstandings and prejudices from the mainland of Britain and beyond, and dismiss the dominant role of religion as the weakness of a simple people who don't know any better, in the grip of overbearing church structures, and repressed by their priests and ministers. It is true these church leaders exercise power in secular island life which can be far from positive, having eroded much of the traditional musical culture from the Protestant isles, for instance. And the community does impose high expectations on the behaviour of church members. But the faith is closely tied to the islands' culture and Gaelic language, and can barely be judged by reference to mainland standards.

One of the most striking aspects of religion in the outer isles is the sharp divide between the Protestants who dominate to north of Benbecula and the Roman Catholics who are just as dominant in the south. (The presence of the British military between the two is, it should be said, purely coincidental.) In the south, the faith and culture appear to be similar to the west of Ireland, but unlike most of Scotland's Catholics, who live in west central Scotland, the Catholicism is not the result of Irish immigration. It dates back to pre-Reformation times, when followers of St Columba on Iona travelled throughout the islands spreading Christianity. In the early 17th century, the Roman church was not allowed to organise on the islands, and the people of the southern isles were resistant to conversion. In Barra, for instance, travellers noted that the people had kept a belief in Saint Finbarr, so the Roman Catholic church gradually regained a foothold when priests became established.

The Protestants from Benbecula northwards have developed a more distinctive approach, unlike anything else in the world – though visitors from smalltown, Bible-belt America may notice some similarities, perhaps based on a common Scots-Irish ancestry. The outward signs of the church influence are clear, especially on a Sunday, when many on the northern isles observe the Lord's Day with solemn reverence, prayer and bible reading. The children's swings in Stornoway's playpark are famously padlocked on the Sabbath, and it can be difficult for the visitor to get food or any other service. And even the large, but rather cowed, minority who are not church-goers accept this as part of their culture, though it can reportedly be very frustrating for irreligious teenagers.

Other signs come from the people of the northern isles: generally reserved, quiet, dignified, warm and with a pawky humour. Their social lives are not carried out in public and in pubs, making the townships seem often lifeless to an outsider. But there can be a lively interchange between people's homes, with the occasional dram, great story-telling and ferocious gossip. They also tend to have a disturbingly keen interest in ecclesiastical history, strengthening the impression that island culture and faith are closely linked.

from *Scottish Island Hopping* (1994)

Donald Macphie (b. 1852)

The Communion Season in the Island
Skye

It is about this time of the year that the service of the Lord's Supper used to be held in many areas of the Highlands, and there is no other religious service that will endure so long in the memories of the people nor one that will leave a savour so fragrant after it. It arouses a particular reverence among young and old such as will rarely be found elsewhere.

Let us consider this day – the Fast Day – as it used to be held. Most of the people prepare for it as though it were the Sabbath itself. The residents of the lower part of the Parish – at least the elderly – must make preparation for the road. The man who would have a cart and a garron would give an invitation to any one who would be too frail to walk. As for young lads and girls, walking ten or a dozen miles would not put any bother on them.

The church will be full with a congregation, peaceable and sedate. It is a minister from the people of another parish who will be preaching, and certainly he is the one who needs to be careful lest a single syllable falls from his lips to give offence to the worthy folk who are sitting near the pulpit, or in the circle of the elders.

Before the minister gives an invitation to the table to the flock whose will it is to partake fittingly of the Lord's Supper, he declares fearlessly the marks of people who are suited and of the ones are not. It is then that anxiety of spirit begins among the communicants and it is no wonder though they would be considering themselves unworthy of the privilege, after listening to fiery words. But prayer will hasten the bidding, and while the psalm is being sung, one man will come forward, quietly, by himself. The rest will follow him in the same way, and the solemn service will commence. No customs are followed besides the simple practice of the first supper, and no flourishes of any sort are seen. Everything is simple and in due order.

Translated from Gaelic by Hugh Cheape, National Museums of Scotland

(*Note: In the large parishes of the Highlands and Islands it was deemed desirable to avoid frequent communion and to concentrate on a single celebration in the year. The 'season' of Holy Communion would generally be fixed for the early summer, between the end of spring work and the beginning of harvest. These were public occasions and were attended by large numbers, moving in from other parishes in the Presbytery from the Wednesday preceding the Sacrament and clearly had their social as well as spiritual advantages.*)

Sign,
Trumpan, Skye.

Alexander Carmichael

In Barra, lots are cast for the *iolachan iasgaich* (fishing-banks), on Bride's Day. These fishing-banks of the sea are as well known and as accurately defined by the fishermen of Barra as are the qualities and boundaries of their crofts on land, and they apportion them with equal care. Having ascertained among themselves the number of boats going to the long-line fishing, the people divide the banks accordingly.

All go to church on St Bride's Day. After reciting the virtues and blessings of Bride, and the examples to be drawn from her life, the priest reminds his hearers that the great God who made the land and all thereon, also made the sea and all therein, and that *cuilidh Chaluim agus cuilidh Mhoire* (the treasury of Columba and the treasury of Mary, that is, the wealth of sea and the plenty of land) are His gift to them that follow Him and call upon His name, on rocky hill or on crested wave. The priest urges upon them to avoid disputes and quarrels over their fishing, to remember the dangers of the deep and the precariousness of life, and in their fishing to remember the poor, the widow and the orphan, now left to the fatherhood of God and to the care of His people. Having come out of church, the men cast lots for the fishing-banks at the church door. After this, they disperse to their homes, all talking loudly and discussing their luck or unluck in the drawing of the lots. A stranger would be apt to think that the people were quarrelling. But it is not so. The simultaneous talking is their habit, and the loudness of their speaking is the necessity of their living among the noise of winds and waves, whether on sea or on shore.

from *Carmina Gadelica, Ortha nan Gaidheal* (1900)

Christina Shaw

Harris

And if the waulking was on Hallowe'en there was no rest for them. They are out all night. When the waulking was over they used to go together to some house. They would be outside first; they would go into the kailyards and they would steal cabbage and anything they liked to take from there. They would go to the windows and they would splash water on the windows. And they would go to the stackyards and they used to pull straws out and count how many grains were on leach of the straws, and that was the number of children they were to have. And the house in which Hallowe'en was kept, all kinds of food were placed before them. There would be a feast of food, meat and boiled potatoes and everything. But anyway, plates would be set on a table with salt in one, meal in one, and – I can't remember what other things they used to have. And the girl who but – they would be blindfolded – and they came and put their hand at random in one or other of the plates. Anyway, the one who put her hand in the plate with salt in it, she was to marry a fisherman and the one who put her hand in the plate with meal in it, she was to marry a farmer. And – oh, I can't remember what else, there were masses of things they did. And finally they went with a ball – they made a ball of rope and they threw into a pitch dark barn, and they would shout in the doorway, 'Who is but there at the end of my rope?' And most likely one of the boys would have gone into the barn so as to be ready to catch the rope, and someone would shout, 'It's me – Murdo!' or 'It's me – Alasdair!' and that was the me she was going to marry.

And they went out with a spade, you know, and they cut a divot out of the ground and they put the divot back again, secretly, and pretty often there would be a slug or a worm there when they went in the morning to see if anything had appeared there. And if – the girl who found that a beetle or anything had appeared in the hole she'd taken the divot out of, she was certain to marry before the end of the year, and when there was no beastie or anything in the hole, there was no hope for that one . . .

And there was such dancing and singing along with that too.

MMcL: With Hallowe'en?

CS: Yes, until nearly daylight . . .

At first it was only the girls. It was the girls who should have been keeping Hallowe'en on their own, but later the boys started to join them. They used to invite them to join them, the same way as Hogmanay was left to the boys. In all the time when I was young none of the girls went with the boys collecting for the New Year. Well, the boys had Hogmanay and the girls had Hallowe'en to themselves, but latterly they started to join together and oh, it was better, it was more enjoyable when the boys were in with them. And so, that's how it was.

from *Tocher* 41

New Year Guising in Lewis

Donald MacDonald

We had it on Christmas night, but it was very often held any time between Christmas Eve and Hogmanay . . . With us anyway it was the Christmas Eve or as near as possible . . . I was never the leader; I was the one who did the chanting for my group . . . from the time I was about nine or so . . . I was one of a band: we always looked forward to being old enough to join a band, usually when we were about seven.

AB: And then what was the oldest that they would go?

DM: Just about fifteen, shortly after leaving school; they left school at fourteen in these days . . . There was very little after 1919. The War, the First World War, more or less put a stop to this.

AB: And . . . this happened in most of the villages in Lewis?

DM: At one time in every village, not only in Lewis, but through . . . the Highlands and the Islands as well . . .

Well, the skin was either a dried sheepskin or a dried calfskin with a loop . . . attached to it that went round your neck, so that the skin hung down your back.

AB: And who carried that?

DM: That was the leader, that was his job . . . The rest of us . . . we had willow staves, and we beat on that as we went through the village – just the noise, but we always made sure we hit the . . . hide in such a way that we did not hurt the wearer . . . We gave it slanting blows . . . but the dried skin gave out quite a loud noise.

AB: And in a big village there could be more than one lot going?

DM: Oh yes, the number of bands depended on the size of the village. I belonged to a band in the north end of my own village, but there were other two at least in the southern end, which was a bigger area. But we made sure that the area that each band visited didn't overlap somebody else's area, because it wouldn't do for two different groups to go to the same house.

AB: . . . And you'd be about . . . between ten and twenty in a band?

DM: Yes, you can say it averaged about fifteen – ten to twenty . . . because, well . . . it was a compact band of the children who lived near one another . . . Most of us . . . visited their parents' homes during the evening.

AB: And it was in the evening that you went out, after dark?

DM: Oh yes, after dark. And it is dark early, it's dark in Lewis about four o'clock at Christmas time.

AB: And how late would you go on?

DM: Until we finished eating as much as we could! Ten-ish, anyway . . . Every house in that district, in that area that we had, we'd call at, because if you didn't, the wives – the housewives were very annoyed because it meant, if you omitted one, it meant you thought they were a wee bit mean; and no housewife would like to be looked on as . . . that kind of person. And not only that . . . you wouldn't leave [out] your own mother's house if you could possibly help it, because she'd have something special because you were there.

AB: And you chanted the rhyme in front of each door.

DM: Yes, and then when the door was opened we chanted it inside as well. We didn't open the door, the door was opened for us . . . The fire in these days in . . . most houses was in the middle of the floor. If there was a chimney, there was a chair placed as near the middle of the floor as possible. And you walked thrice sunwise round the . . . fire, chanting as you went along, and all the occupants of the house tried to hit that hide – why, I've no idea – with sticks, with the tongs even (an old lady, I remember an old lady using the tongs): those who had no . . . implement, if you can call it such, to hit it with, they used their hands. It was part of the ceremony that they had to do this touching of the skin, this hitting of the skin. And after the rhyme was chanted, the housewife had all her – gifts, if you like – prepared, and they were put into the clean flour sack. We usually had – very often two sacks, just to be on the safe side . . . Not an ordinary sack, but a flour sack, which . . . could be cleaned very well . . .

Each village had . . . a slightly different rhyme, but there were words, phrases that belonged to . . . the whole island. But they were variations from village to village, in the rune chanted.

AB: I see. Now what did you call it in Gaelic?

DM: The night? *Oidhche nam Bonnag*, the Night of the Gifts . . . No, it's not bannocks, that's *Bannach*.

AB: But what did you call the rhyme?

DM: Duan – Duan nam Bonnag.

It started off with *Hurra bhith ó*, a phrase that means nothing, but it was spoken by the crowd before the . . . *duan* leader started . . . before each line . . .

AB: It was always chanted, it was never sung?

DM: No, it was just chanted like that.

AB: And everybody would join in with the Hurra b hith ó*?*

DM: . . . Like the Greek chorus!

AB: And then . . . after you'd collected as much as you could, then you adjourned.

DM: Adjourned. We usually chose as ... shall we say, the guest-house, a house where an old maid lived by herself, and we usually went back to the same house year after year. And she entered into the fun of the thing very well indeed. She collected spoons, she collected cups, she'd collect tables if necessary and chairs, anything that she felt we needed. And she made sure that the windows were curtained off, so that no person could peep in and see. So ... when we'd visited all the houses we had to visit, we came to her, and she took charge then, with the senior boy or boys, to give each person as much as possible. But she paid particular attention to the young boys, to make sure that they got their share; and she also took part, and anything that was left over, it was all given to her afterwards ... The one we went visiting, she was the school cleaner ... well, she was used to children all her life, and she certainly looked after us very well indeed ...

Now, did we have tea? I think we must have; yes, we must have, ... at least in my time; probably before that it was milk they would have, but we had tea. And later on fruit was given, but that was something new: when I was a wee boy we didn't have much in the way of fruit ... Bannocks, scones, and the odd loaf, because, oh, a loaf was very precious ...

The boys and girls went round at [Hallowe'en], but only boys at Christmas-time ... We just went as we were ... We had nothing to dress up in!

from *Tocher*

A Belief in Fairies

Nan MacKinnon
Vatersay

So in the old days there was a belief in the fairies?

Oh, they all believed in the fairies. The fairies weren't near the towns. They were out in the lonely districts. Out in the moors. They weren't near the houses.

They were supernatural. They had their own power. They could sing and dance. They were very musical and could dance to the music of the bagpipes. Bagpipes were their only musical instrument.

When you were little, what stories were popular among the children?

Yes, about the fairies and all that. And children wandering away from home and the fairies getting a hold of them and all this . . . They say they are here for a century and away for another century. This is their century away.

What about a woman being stolen by the fairies with marriage in mind?

Oh, there were the women. They did their best to entice them over to their own fairyland . . . They never enticed the men. It was the men came after the girls. It's the way I heard it anyway.

Was there any fear of the fairies? Were people worried going out late at night? What about the shepherds?

In my day there weren't as many shepherds about. The land was cut up into farms. But before that they used to meet the fairies and courted them and all the rest of it. Whether that's true or not . . . You just couldn't say to anybody that was telling you a story about fairies that he said he actually saw, you couldn't just turn around and say that wasn't true. You'd never say that. So the stories went on from time to time. So there must have been something – supposing a few old people were imagining, they couldn't all have been imagining . . .

from *Tocher* 42

The Smith and the Fairies

Rev. Thomas Pattieson
Islay

Years ago there lived in Crossbrig a smith of the name of MacEachern. This man had an only child, a boy of about thirteen or fourteen years of age, cheerful, strong, and healthy. All of a sudden he fell ill; took to his bed and moped whole days away. No one could tell what was the matter with him, and the boy himself could not, or would not, tell how he felt. He was wasting away fast; getting thin, old, and yellow; and his father and all his friends were afraid that he would die.

At last one day, after the boy had been lying in this condition for a long time, getting neither better nor worse, always confined to bed, but with an extraordinary appetite, – one day, while sadly revolving these things, and standing idly at his forge, with no heart to work, the smith was agreeably surprised to see an old man, well known to him for his sagacity and knowledge of out-of-the-way things, walk into his workshop. Forthwith he told him the occurrence which had clouded his life.

The old man looked grave as he listened; and after sitting a long time pondering over all he had heard, gave his opinion thus – 'It is not your son you have got. The boy has been carried away by the 'Daoine Sith,' and they have left a *Sibhreach* in his place.' 'Alas! and what then am I to do?' said the smith. 'How am I ever to see my own son again?' 'I will tell you how,' answered the old man. 'But, first, to make sure that it is not your own son you have got, take as many empty egg shells as you can get, go with them into the room, spread them out carefully before his sight, then proceed to draw water with them, carrying them two and two in your hands as if they were a great weight, and arrange when full, with every sort of earnestness round the fire,' The smith accordingly gathered as many broken egg-shells as he could get, went into the room, and proceeded to carry out all his instructions.

He had not been long at work before there arose from the bed a shout of laughter, and the voice of the seeming sick boy exclaimed, 'I am now 800 years of age, and I have never seen the like of that before.'

The smith returned and told the old man, 'Well, now,' said the sage to him, 'did I not tell you that it was not your son you had: your son is in Brorra-cheill in a digh there (that is, a round green hill frequented by fairies). Get rid as soon as possible of this intruder, and I think I may promise you your son.'

'You must light a very large and bright fire before the bed on which this stranger is lying. He will ask you 'What is the use of such a fire as that?' Answer him at once, 'You will see that presently!' and then seize him, and throw him into the middle of it. If it is your own son you have got, he will call out to save him; but if not, this thing will fly through the roof.'

The smith again followed the old man's advice; kindled a large fire, answered the question put to him as he had been directed to do, and seizing the child flung him in without hesitation. The 'Sibhreach' gave an awful yell, and sprung through the roof, where a hole was left to let the smoke out.

On a certain night the old man told him the green round hill, where the fairies kept the boy, would be open. And on that night the smith, having provided himself with a bible, a dirk, and a crowing cock, was to proceed to the hill. He would hear singing and dancing and much merriment going on, but he was to advance boldly; the bible he carried would be a certain safeguard to him against any danger from the fairies. On entering the hill he was to stick the dirk in the threshold, to prevent the hill from closing upon him; 'and then,' continued the old man, 'on entering you will see a spacious apartment before you, beautifully clean, and there, standing far within, working at a forge, you will also see your own son. When you are questioned, say you come to seek him, and will not go without him.'

Not long after this, the time came round, and the smith sallied forth, prepared as instructed. Sure enough as he approached the hill, there was a light where light was seldom seen before. Soon after a sound of piping, dancing, and joyous merriment reached the anxious father on the night wind.

Overcoming every impulse to fear, the smith approached the threshold steadily, stuck the dirk into it as directed, and entered. Protected by the bible he carried on his breast, the fairies could not touch him; but they asked him, with a good deal of displeasure, what he wanted there. He answered, 'I want my son, whom I see down there, and I will not go without him.'

Upon hearing this, the whole company before him gave a loud laugh, which wakened up the cock he carried dozing in his arms, who at once leaped up on his shoulders, clapped his wings lustily, and crowed loud and long.

The fairies, incensed, seized the smith and his son, and throwing them out of the hill, flung the dirk after them, 'and in an instant a' was dark.'

For a year and a day the boy never did a turn of work, and hardly ever spoke a word; but at last one day, sitting by his father and watching him finishing a sword he was making for some chief, and which he was very particular about, he suddenly exclaimed, 'That is not the way to do it;' and taking the tools from his father's hands he set to work himself in his place, and soon fashioned a sword, the like of which was never seen in the country before.

From that day the young man wrought constantly with his father, and became the inventor of a peculiarly fine and well-tempered weapon, the making of which kept the two smiths, father and son, in constant employment, spread their fame far and wide, and gave them the means in abundance, as they before had the disposition to live content with all the world and very happily with one another.

from *Popular Tales of the West Highlands, Vol I* (1860)

Herding Blessing

Mrs Morrison

That's a Herding Blessing . . . as we called it . . . There used to be a cattle-fold in these days . . . and you had to have a pail. And you sat by the cow milking her and you started to sing the song and no matter how wild she was, the cow would stand still for you when she heard the song . . . When they went to the fold they always had some song or other for the cows and the cows used to lick them. But today all they get is a kick. There's no word of a song.

from *Tocher* 7

Cattle on the beach, South Harris, 1951.

Copyright acknowledgements

E. Mairi MacArthur: extract from *Columba's Island* (EUP, 1995). Reprinted by permission of the author.

Sorley Maclean: 'Hallaig' from *Reothairt is Contraigh* (Canongate Publishers, 1977). Reprinted by permission of the publishers.

Francis Thompson: extracts from *Crofting Years* (Luath Press, 1984). Reprinted by permission of the publishers.

Ben Buxton: extract from *Mingulay* (Birlinn, 1995). Reprinted by permission of the publishers.

Thomas A. Clark: 'A Crofter's Garden'. Reprinted by permission of the author.

'TV Show makes German Laird of Dun Maraig' from *The West Highland Free Press*. Reprinted by permission of the publisher.

Brian Jackman: extract from the introduction to *Sula: The Seabird Hunters of Lewis* by John Beatty (Michael Joseph, 1992). Reprinted by permission of the publishers.

Johanna MacDonald: extract from *Country Bairns: Growing Up 1900–1930* (EUP, 1992). Reprinted by permission of the publishers.

Margaret Fay Shaw: extracts from *Folksongs and Folklore of South Uist* (Routledge and Kegan Paul Ltd, 1977). Reprinted by permission of the author. Extract from *From the Alleghenies to the Hebrides* (Canongate Books, 1993). Reprinted by permission of the publishers.

Calum Johnston: extract from *Tocher* 10. Reprinted by permission of the School of Scottish Studies.

Hugh MacKinnon: 'Shinty in Eigg' from *Tocher*. Reprinted by permission of the School of Scottish Studies.

Eric Cregeen and Donald W. MacKenzie: extract from *Tiree Bards and their Bardachd* (Society of West Highland and Island Historical Research, 1978). Reprinted by permission of the publishers.

William Matheson: extract from *The Blind Harper: The songs of Roderick Morison and his music* (The Scottish Gaelic Texts Society, 1970). Reprinted by permission of the Society and Scottish Academic Press.

Colm O Baoill: extract from *Eachann Bacach and other Maclean poets* (The Scottish

Mrs Christina Shaw: extracts from *Tocher* 30 and *Tocher* 41. Reprinted by permission of the School of Scottish Studies.

Donald MacDonald: 'New Year Guising in Lewis' from *Tocher*. Reprinted by permission of the School of Scottish Studies.

Nan MacKinnon: 'A Belief in Fairies' from *Tocher* 42. Reprinted by permission of the School of Scottish Studies.

The editors would like to thank the following for agreeing to be interviewed and their material used in this book. Interviews carried out by Margaret Bennett and Michael Newton.

Chrissie Oliver
John Grant
Peigi Stewart

The Editors

Marion Sinclair was brought up on the Island of Barra in the Outer Hebrides and was educated there and on the Isle of Lewis. She now lives and works in Edinburgh and is the editor of *Scottish Island Hopping: A Guide for the Independent Traveller* and co-editor of *Scottish Love Stories*.

Since coming to Scotland from America **Michael Newton** has done field work among Gaels on the Scottish mainland and islands. He is currently researching the relationship between Gaels and their land for a doctorate at the Celtic department of Edinburgh University.